Supernatural Encounters

True Paranormal Accounts from Law Enforcement

Elliott Van Dusen

Foreword by Darryll Walsh

Published by IngramSpark Content
www.ingramspark.com

ISBN: 978-1-9991385-2-3

Book cover design by Cody Hess and Krusher Design

Dedication

I dedicate this book to all of my brothers and sisters in law enforcement who selflessly sacrifice their own wellness and responsibilities in the interest of public safety.

I also dedicate this book to my favourite person, Sarah Crawley. Your continual love, support and encouragement pulls me from the dark. May our love remain everlasting luminescent throughout time.

To my daughters Sofia and Meadow, you are the most wonderful gift a father could ask for. I eternally love you both. And finally;

My mother Kim Farrell who encouraged me to write another book about the spirits who haunt humankind.

Acknowledgements

I would like to thank Darryll Walsh, Paul Campbell, Steven MacLean, Andrew Baird, Patrick Murphy, Rob McGinley, Jim Blackwood, Jason Murphy and those who wished to remain anonymous for bringing some of these stories to my attention. You exemplify Paranormal Phenomena Research & Investigation's motto of bringing the truth to the light.

Finally, a special thank you to Sarah Crawley for her editing assistance.

Matthew 5:9

"Blessed are the peacemakers, for they shall be called sons of God."

Table of Contents

FOREWARD

...if you gaze for long into an abyss, the abyss gazes also into you.

Friedrich Nietzsche

One must be prepared to look into many an abyss- or perhaps more accurately, rabbit hole- when trying to fathom truth and illusion in the paranormal. A stout heart and eager mind are also requisite for the much more tedious, boring, and difficult job of a paranormal researcher than commonly portrayed online or in popular media.

Ever since I have known Elliott Van Dusen his greatest hero was someone who had a stout heart and eager mind, *Fox Mulder*. And Van Dusen has, not only the same qualities as his hero, he has succeeded in becoming Canada's Fox Mulder through his studies, investigations, and training as an RCMP officer.

Though it took Fox Mulder six seasons to understand often not everything is as it seems in the paranormal, Van Dusen came to this realization much sooner and this has made him a superior investigator, with the skills of a parapsychologist and RCMP officer intertwined. These two qualities also make for a superior writer and the perfect author of a book on this topic. An author who has the experience and training of both occupations is more authentic and genuine than the one who just relates a story as he might read the items off a menu. It takes more effort and intellect than most writers in this field demonstrate in order to tease reality out from under the cloak of illusion and capture the intricacies of any one case.

I am certain you will enjoy this book, and it might just help you determine the boundaries of illusion and reality for yourself.

- **Darryll B. D. Walsh, Parapsychologist and Executive Director of the Centre for Parapsychological Studies in Canada**

INTRODUCTION

In my younger years while studying criminology at Saint Mary's University in Halifax, Nova Scotia, and parapsychology from institutions around the world, I never anticipated the two disciplines would eventually lead me to writing this book. The disciplines do however, have some commonalities.

Criminology and parapsychology are both interdisciplinary social sciences. Despite the misconception, parapsychology is not a pseudo-science. It is recognized by the American Association for the Advancement of Science as a social science. While criminology is the study of crime as a social phenomenon, parapsychology is the study of extrasensory perception, mind-matter interaction and survival after bodily death and how it associates to human experiences as a social phenomenon.

For as long as I can remember, I have been fascinated with hauntings and anything to do with the supernatural. My first exposure to the paranormal was through the television series *Unsolved Mysteries*. In 1997, Mark Cameron and I created a paranormal investigative group called Paranormal Phenomena Research & Investigation (PPRI). To this day, PPRI is still an active, non-profit organization in which I serve as the Corporate Director.

In 2000, my mother showed me a newspaper clipping from the Chronicle Herald about a Halifax parapsychologist named Dr. Darryll Walsh who was teaching parapsychology courses at the Nova Scotia Community College. It was in November 2000 when I enrolled in one of Dr. Walsh's courses commencing my long journey into formal parapsychology training.

After completing Parapsychology I: Predictions and Predictors and Parapsychology II: Apparitions and Near-Death Experiences, I was invited to join the Centre for Parapsychological Studies in Canada where Dr. Walsh served as the Executive Director. The Centre was a non-profit parapsychological investigative team which investigated hauntings and other parapsychological phenomena throughout Atlantic Canada.

Under Dr. Walsh's leadership, I learned the tradecraft of being a parapsychological investigator. I have participated in several haunting investigations, conducted parapsychology research and assisted in teaching parapsychology at the Nova Scotia Community College. I have also participated in film documentaries, newspaper and radio interviews. In 2001, I earned a diploma in Parapsychology from the Stratford Career Institute. In 2004, I completed a non-accredited Doctor of Philosophy degree in Parapsychology from the American International University.

In January 2005, I was recruited out of Saint Mary's University by the Royal Canadian Mounted Police (RCMP). I left Halifax to attend their six-month Cadet Training Program in Regina, Saskatchewan. As a fifteen-year veteran with the RCMP I spent nine and a half years investigating homicides, sex crimes and other violent crimes. For the first thirteen years of my career, I was publicly unaffiliated with the paranormal but continued to read newspaper articles, watch television documentaries and study parapsychology in private.

I have been fortunate enough to study under some highly

respected individuals in the field of parapsychology. In 2011, I completed a parapsychology course taught by Dr. Caroline Watt from the University of Edinburgh's Koestler Parapsychology Unit. In 2018 and 2019 I successfully completed three eight-week courses from the Rhine Education Center under parapsychologist Loyd Auerbach. The three courses were entitled Field Investigations of Apparitions, Hauntings and Poltergeists, Advanced Field Investigations and a Scientific Approach to Extrasensory Perception. In July 2020, I completed Eight Important Studies in Parapsychology taught by the Executive Director of the Rhine Research Center, John Kruth. I was invited to sit on the Rhine Research Team consisting of some of the top researchers in the field of parapsychology.

This book is nonfiction and the events contained herein are completely true. Due to the inherent nature of policing, namely safety and security concerns along with the dysfunctional policing culture, in which I can relate, some of the officers wished to remain anonymous and expressed great concern surrounding their privacy and the potential for disruptive activity. Much like my favourite television character *Fox Mulder* from *The X-Files,* we share the common bond of being recipients of ridicule from co-workers due to our involvement with the paranormal. As a result, I have been periodically and maliciously harassed.

I have therefore taken these concerns into consideration and have respected them throughout the writing process. Some of the officers, witnesses and their organizations involved in this book have been given pseudonyms and purposely withheld, strictly for privacy reasons. I wish to advise readers that by protecting the safety and privacy of certain individuals, it has no bearing on the validity of the events or testimony of the individuals.

People have been experiencing apparitions and hauntings for centuries, however, parapsychological investigations and research didn't formally commence until the early 1800's with Franz Anton Mesmer. Mesmer was a German doctor who developed mesmerism which in turn led to the development of hypnosis. Early society also did not have organized police forces to conduct criminal investigations and citizens were tasked with the responsibility of policing themselves. They would patrol their communities in an attempt to thwart any criminal activity. Occasionally, these unofficial law enforcement officers would experience ghostly apparitions while on patrol.

It is time to put your seatbelt on, because you are riding shotgun with me while I take you on patrol discussing true historic and contemporary supernatural encounters witnessed by law enforcement personnel.

THE BUSH MAN

Approximately 164 kilometers northwest of the City of Yellowknife, nestled into the boreal forest,` is the small indigenous community of Whatí in the spectacular Northwest Territories, Canada. This small isolated community is home to approximately 500 people. The community has always been home to an abundant of wildlife including fish, wolves, black bears, caribou and eagles. This is no surprise, considering the vast land mass and abundance of forested land in the area. There is however, another creature which has been said to roam Whatí. The local indigenous people call it Nàhgą, or in English, the Bush Man.

The Bush Man has been described by locals and witnesses as being a hairy ape-like creature that walks upright and dwells in the forests surrounding Whatí. The indigenous people of the region believe the Bush Man is responsible for the disappearance of children and bush camp workers. Having worked the Northwest Territories divisional homicide unit for three years, there are a number of outstanding missing persons in the territory. In the majority of the cases, good enough circumstances existed for investigators to make an educated guess on what happened to the missing individual. However, there was the odd missing person who would vanish without a trace. The Bush Man is believed to be a type of Bigfoot or Sasquatch. Folklorists have traced the stories of Bigfoot as far back as medieval times in Europe. The belief is strongest in North American and Native American folklore.

In the winter of 2007, Sergeant Peter Starzky was posted to

the Whatí RCMP Detachment. Sgt. Starzky was working as a young Constable at the time with only one other police officer. Whatí was only a two person detachment. When officers are not scheduled to work, they are placed on call in the event that a citizen would require police assistance. One evening while Sgt. Starzky was at home in bed, he received a call for service. A dispatcher from the Yellowknife telecommunications center told Sgt. Starzky that a citizen was requesting a patrol because he believed that the Bush Man was outside his residence. Sgt. Starzky staggered out of bed, grabbed his duty belt and fired up the police truck.

Upon arriving at the scene, Sgt. Starzky checked the perimeter of the residence for signs of a trespasser. He noted that the snow on the property had not been disturbed. Sgt. Starzky knocked on the door of the residence until he was greeted by a frightened complainant. Sgt. Starzky told the complainant that he had checked the exterior of his property, but had seen no signs of a trespasser. The complainant told Sgt. Starzky that he had seen the Bush Man near his windows. Sgt. Starzky being the no nonsense, rough and tough Mountie that he is, boldly told the complainant that there were no footprints near any of his windows. The complainant looked at Sgt. Starzky like he had lost his mind and said "The Bush Man doesn't leave footprints!" Sgt. Starzky assured him that there was no trespasser on his property and wished him a good evening. Sgt. Starxky did not note any signs of drug or alcohol use.

Sgt. Starzky was involved with one more incident involving the Bush Man during his posting in Whatí. It was during the day time and he was on patrol in the community. Suddenly there was a large commotion occurring amongst the locals. Sgt. Starzky could hear a bell being rung and people running toward the Community School. Sgt. Starzky stopped his police truck and asked one of the locals what was going on. The local told Sgt. Starzky that someone in the community had spotted the Bush Man on the outskirts of Whatí and that community members were rounding up all of the children in the community so that the Bush Man wouldn't steal any of them. Sgt. Starzky assured the local resident that no one was going to steal any child but that didn't persuade the community members. Sgt. Starzky patrolled the community while everyone was hunkered down, but he saw no signs of the Bush Man.

Sgt. Starzky transferred out of Whatí, but Bush Man sightings have continued. On July 17, 2016 Whatí resident Tony Williah was boating near the most northern tip of Lac La Marte when he spotted some garbage floating in the water ahead of him. As he reached down to grab the garbage from the water, a wave rocked his boat so hard that he fell backward into the freezing water. He was unable to get back into his boat, so he grabbed his supply bag and struggled to swim to shore. He eventually made it to an island at the end of the point, feeling somewhat relieved. However, shortly after his arrival, he saw what he believed to be the Bush Man standing beside him. The Bush Man darted off into the bushes and Williah could hear branches breaking. Terrified, Williah grabbed his bag and jumped back into the water swimming away from the island. Williah spent another 48 hours alone in the wilderness until he was rescued by the RCMP and Canadian Armed Forces.

DORCHESTER PENITENTIARY

Our next stop takes us to Dorchester Penitentiary situated in Dorchester, New Brunswick. Dorchester penitentiary is an all-male, multi-level security institution which has been in operation since July 14, 1880 making it the second oldest continuously operating correctional facility in Canada. It has the capability to house 699 prisoners.

Correctional Officer Walter Bearon has worked for Correctional Service Canada for the past 10 years. Like most emergency workers, Officer Bearon was often required to work the backshift.

According to Officer Bearon, there was an inmate murdered at the Dorchester Penitentiary. In parapsychological studies, there is a commonality between sudden, accidental or unexpected deaths and hauntings. Individuals who die expectedly due to illness or under normal conditions are more apt to move on and less likely to remain behind.

The staff who have worked Dorchester Penitentiary claim that the troubled soul keeps a watchful eye out on the range. The range is a term used to describe the cell block which houses prisoners. He has been known to wake up napping Correctional Officers ensuring that they make their rounds, preventing any potential harm to prisoners. Hopefully one day his soul can finally rest. In the meantime, he continues to pay his debt to society.

BEAVERBANK, NOVA SCOTIA UFO SIGHTING

Situated at 125 Knowles Crescent in Beaverbank, Nova Scotia is Scotia Nursing Home. It was built within an area commonly referred to as the Beaverbank Villa. The Beaverbank area of Nova Scotia has a rich history of reported supernatural occurrences including ghostly apparitions, UFO and strange creature sightings. Scotia Nursing Home is one of the only buildings which still remain at the location.

A patrol through the area today reveals only the scars of a ghostly village which was once a thriving military community. Overgrown plant vegetation and deteriorated roadways are all that remains as Mother Nature slowly reclaims what is rightfully hers.

Beaverbank Villa wasn't always like this though. In 1953, the Royal Canadian Air Force and United States Air Force built RCAF Station Beaverbank which was a long-range early warning radar station. It was in operation up until January 1, 1964 at which time it briefly became a cement factory. All of the accommodations which used to house military personnel were demolished in 2004. The RCAF Station Beaverbank building, although in very derelict condition, still stands at the top of the hill and is accessible only by foot or on an all-terrain vehicle.

On April 23, 2004 Paranormal Phenomena Research & Investigation investigators Adam Myles, Dave Myles, Chad Murphy and myself were following up on reported haunting activity at the abandoned RCAF Station Beaverbank building. As we were exiting the building, all four of us noticed several lights in the East, including a moving red light which was bobbing up and down for several minutes. Adam tried to record the incident on video, however, the battery in the camera suddenly died. Adam switched to his fully charged backup battery as Dave, Chad and myself watched intently as the red glowing light continued to bob up and down in a way that known conventional aircraft cannot do. As Adam loaded the fully charged battery into his camcorder, that too suddenly died. Electronic disturbances and failure of electronics are a common occurrence during a UFO sighting.

Suddenly a second red light swooped in which promoted the first red light to ascend upwards and fly over the second red light. The two red lights then ascended at an extremely high rate of speed and disappeared above into the atmosphere. At the time of this event, people did not have cell phone cameras. I had an old Audiovox cellphone and where the two batteries for the camcorder died, we were unable to get any video or photographs of the UFO sighting.

The following day I began conducting some follow up investigation in order to rule out any natural phenomena. I called Transport Canada and reported the incident. I asked if there was a flight path over the area in which we had seen the unidentified flying object, however, this was post 9/11 terror attacks. Transport Canada advised that flight paths were considered Top Secret information that couldn't be released.

I conducted further investigation through the use of the Internet and was able to determine that it wasn't weather phenomena, satellites or any other astronomical phenomena passing through the area at the time of the sighting. I also reported the incident to the Canadian UFO Report which catalogs UFO sightings across Canada. They conducted some follow up as well and were unable to explain the sighting. For all intents and purposes, the UFO sighting, "unidentified flying object" remains unexplained.

A HAUNTING IN KENTVILLE

Let's grab a coffee and keep on patrolling because we have many more cases which need to be explored. Our next encounter is another field investigation that I conducted. It was at a private residence in the small Nova Scotia town of Kentville.

On June 14, 2004 I was contacted by Shaylene Tucker who was looking for assistance with her newly purchased home. She and her husband had only lived in the residence for seven months when they began experiencing some unusual phenomena. The house was built in the 1920's and was renovated with some of the original wood work coming from the old Canadian Pacific Hotel in Kentville.

Mrs. Tucker told me about some of the strange events she had experienced. She said she had a small video of what she believed to be a bouncing orb of light taken off of her back step. She also had a photograph which contained the image of what appeared to be the face of an indigenous looking man. Mrs. Tucker also described seeing a dark shadow walk down the hall while she was sitting in the living room.

On one particular evening, she was in the kitchen getting ready for bed when she looked toward the patio door and saw a man standing there. Scared, she yelled for her husband to come to the kitchen. She asked where the camera was and Mr. Tucker said it was in the office. She went to get the camera and tried to take a photo of the man staring at her. When the photograph was developed it didn't contain a picture of a man, but it revealed a hazy image of what appeared to be that of a female. Mrs. Tucker also reported seeing small flashes of light in the house. When she and her husband first moved into the house, they both heard on several nights the sound of someone walking up the first three steps leading toward the upstairs. As soon as they acknowledged that it may be a ghost, it stopped.

Mrs. Tucker had 3 basset hounds, one of which had come from an abusive home. The adopted basset hound had to be put to sleep after it had lashed out at her daughter. Following this devastating event, Mrs. Tucker reported seeing a basset hound apparition that appeared on several occasion which she described being as clear as if it was sitting right next to her. On one occasion, she was in bed and told her female basset hounds that they had to move so her husband could get into bed when he came upstairs. Mrs. Tucker felt a dog do a few turns on the bed before lying down. A few seconds later, her two basset hounds jumped up on the bed and whatever she felt in the bed had disappeared but the sheets had been disturbed.

On June 12, 2004 Mrs. Tucker told one of her bassets, Peaches, who was on the couch in the living room to come to bed. Mrs. Tucker kept telling her to come upstairs to bed, however, the dog refused to move. Mrs. Tucker decided to leave her downstairs and continued on her way to the master bedroom. When she arrived in the master bedroom, Peaches was already upstairs in her bed.

On June 26, 2004 PPRI investigators Brad Mavin, Chad Murphy, Matt Stewart and I traveled to Kentville to conduct an initial field investigation. We arrived in Kentville at 10:45 pm. Mrs. Tucker came out of the house to greet the investigative team. After a short introduction, we began moving some of our equipment into the residence. I explained to Mr. and Mrs. Tucker how the investigation would be conducted and also explained each piece of equipment that the investigative team was going to utilize.

Mrs. Tucker told us that pennies had been appearing all over her house on almost a daily basis since moving into the house. I had seen this kind of haunting activity in one other case file from the United States. Mrs. Tucker said that a penny had materialized near the kitchen sink this evening just prior to the investigative team arriving.

At 11:30 pm, Brad set up a camcorder. However, fifteen minutes after setting it up, the freshly charged battery died. As with UFO sightings, it is common during haunting investigations to have electronic equipment and batteries malfunction or have their charge rapidly depleted. Brad had a portable camcorder that he reverted too.

At 12:20 pm, Brad told me that the portable camcorder had died after only ten minutes of filming. It seemed to happen after he tried to verbally communicate with any spirits present in hopes of capturing an electronic voice phenomena. He plugged the battery into a wall outlet when suddenly it began sparking. Once the battery was plugged into the wall, it was reading that it was already fully charged.

At 12:25 pm, Mrs. Tucker's daughter said that she had seen something move in the corner of the dining room by one of the chairs. Investigator Chad Murphy took some equipment readings and pictures. There were no anomalous readings on the equipment. However, two rooms over in the office, I got a high reading on the electromagnetic field radiation (EMF) detector. Brad reported feeling as if someone was bouncing up and down in the chair. The EMF reading from the chair lasted for almost 10 minutes, and we were able to rule out that it wasn't radiation emanating from the computer. Eventually, the reading disappeared and we tried to replicate it unsuccessfully.

The topic of "ghost hunting" equipment is a contentious issue in parapsychology. Ghost hunting television shows display a variety of technology that provides the viewer with an entertaining experience but also leaves them with many fallacies. There is field investigation evidence that exists in support of thermometers and electromagnetic field radiation detectors having detected anomalies in the environment when a spirit is believed to be present. There is also an abundance of field investigation evidence which has shown that although someone is experiencing or perceiving a cold or hot spot, often times the equipment is unable to detect a reading. With that being said, there is no conclusive piece of equipment that can accurately and irrefutably detect the presence of a ghost. This is because parapsychologists and other scientists do not know what consciousness is made up of, nor do they know the true environmental effects consciousness has after it leaves the human body.

A study conducted by the late neuropsychologist Dr. Michael Persinger spent a significant amount of time studying the effects of human perception when exposed to electromagnetic radiation. Test subjects subjected to high levels of electromagnetic radiation reported experiencing out of body experiences and saw apparitions and religious figures such as Jesus.

At 1:45 am, Brad was in the upstairs bathroom when he started to get a reading on the EMF detector which also couldn't be duplicated afterward. Two minutes later, I felt a cold spot near the front door and the EMF reader began fluctuating. Once the cold spot dissipated, the EMF reading stopped. I was unable to replicate those readings as well.

At 5:05 am, I went to check the camcorder that was set up in the office. I found an American penny lying next to the dog's food dishes in the kitchen. Both Brad and I had previously searched the area at the start of the evening and the penny was not there previously. Mr. Tucker and the children were in bed at this time and Mrs. Tucker never left the living room with the investigative team. The view of the kitchen area that the investigative team had made it impracticable for someone to fraudulently plant the penny there. The event remained anomalous.

At 7:00 am, we concluded the initial field investigation, rounded up the equipment and departed the residence. Our post investigation analysis didn't turn up any additional proof of paranormal activity either. What was thought to be a possible EVP captured on the micro-cassette recorder turned out to be someone breathing as documented by the video camera. The cold spot, anomalous EMF readings and the penny were the only pieces of evidence we collected during that particular night.

On July 22, 2004, I assembled a larger investigative team

consisting of Brad Mavin, Adam Myles, Chad Murphy, Martin Reid, John Goodwin and myself. I decided to not tell Adam, Martin and John about the specifics of the first field investigation so that they would not have any predetermined biases.

At 6:30 pm, the investigative team arrived at Mr. and Mrs. Tucker's residence. With the commencement of the investigation, some of my investigators detected high EMF readings and a hot spot near the main entrance where I had picked up high readings during my last visit. While in the basement, one of my investigators noticed wiring running along the roof of the basement. The readings were being detected directly above where the wires were running. With the permission of the home owners, we asked if we could turn the power off. Once the power was off, the EMF readings dropped back to 0. When the power was restored, the high readings persisted leading us to the conclusion that the electrical wires were not shielded very well which accounted for the EMF readings near the front door.

While outside, Adam looked through one of the basement windows and saw a black shadow moving over a stool that was sitting near the window. The lights in the basement were off at the time and Adam couldn't make out any specific details. Adam radioed to see if any of the investigators or occupants of the home were in the basement, but everyone was accounted for.

Adam and John were watching the residence with a night vision monocular as it was quite dark outside. John kept seeing a dark figure walk by the upstairs spare bedroom window. John didn't tell Adam this information, but asked him to check the residence himself with the night vision. Adam looked at the house through the night vision and was startled to see a figure walking around the spare bedroom. He contacted the investigators inside the residence to see if anyone was in the upstairs spare room, however, once again everyone was accounted for. Adam passed John the night vision and told him that he was going to go check the room.

As Adam approached the bedroom, the door was closed and there was nobody else upstairs. Adam entered the room which was very small and had a bed situated near the window. There were curtains which were open. He looked at the window and called to John. Out of the corner of his eye, Adam saw a person standing next to him. When he turned to look, he saw a small figure standing on the bed beside him in front of the window. The only noticeable feature he could see was long hair, everything else appeared as a shadow. The apparition disappeared and the lower portion of the curtain drifted up onto the bed.

Adam radioed for any available investigators to come to the spare room. Martin and John came to his aid. Martin noticed that Adam appeared visibly shaken. Adam explained to them what he had witnessed and Martin began using the EMF reader. There were very large EMF readings that kept fluctuating. The investigators began trying to talk to any spirits in the room and asked for them to give a sign if they were present. Adam's two-way radio clicked on its own. Martin is also a Reverend and began leading the investigators in prayer. As they prayed, Adam felt someone put their hand on his shoulder. Initially he was frightened but as Martin continued, his feelings of being afraid changed to that of pure peace and comfort. Adam's knees became weak and he fell down backwards hitting his back on the closet door.

Brad, Chad and I all attended the spare room. Adam told the investigative team that he had a strange feeling about the closet door. There was an EMF reader placed on the bed where Adam had seen the apparition. He opened the door and that very moment, every investigator in the room was overcome with an odd feeling, followed by goosebumps and an icy cold chill which ran right through our chests. It was so powerful that it took away our breath. The EMF reader began going off indicating a change in the electromagnetic environment. Some of the investigators began feeling light headed which persisted for over a minute.

We continued to investigate for a few more hours, but there was no more unusual activity witnessed. The second investigation proved useful in assisting with the conclusion that the residence was most likely haunted and that the haunting wasn't malicious in anyway. We were able to explain the EMF readings near the front door where Mrs. Tucker would hear the sounds of footsteps walking up the stairwell. The high EMF readings near the front door were due to poorly shielded wires from the basement which ran underneath the floor.

However, the appearance of the penny near the dog dishes and the EMF readings from the upstairs washroom and the office remained unexplained. Martin was able to determine that the "indigenous face" which showed up in the door frame picture taken by Mrs. Tucker was as a result of light reflecting off a very smooth, shiny contoured wood frame. The apparition witnessed by Adam and the experiences of the investigators in the spare bedroom also remained unexplained.

HALIFAX SHOPPING CENTRE

Security supervisor Paul Campbell has had some supernatural experiences while working at the Halifax Shopping Centre. Tower 1 and Tower 2 housed corporate and organizational offices and were well known for having strange and unusual events occur amongst the mall staff and tenants. Today, Tower 1 and 2 no longer exist. In 2004, Halifax Shopping Centre underwent a $70 million dollar redevelopment project in which they eliminated office space to make room for additional retail space.

The Victorian Order of Nurses had an office located in Tower 1 of the shopping center. On one particular evening, Campbell was working when one of the nurses attended the security office. The nurse reported that she was using the washroom in Tower 1 when suddenly every stall door began opening and slamming shut violently. Tower 1 was always spooky according to Campbell. The nurse was terrified, so Campbell had her stay in the security office while he and another Security Officer attended the Tower 1 washrooms. Upon inspection of the washrooms, nothing unusual was noted. Campbell spoke with the same nurse about a month later while he was patrolling the mall. The nurse asked him what she could do to make him believe her about the incident. Little did the nurse know that Campbell was also an investigator for the Centre for Parapsychological Studies in Canada, so she couldn't have reported it to a better person.

Tower 2 had some of the mall staff terrified to go near it due to some unusual stories and experiences. The mall's janitorial staff attributed their high turnover rate on the strange phenomena occurring in Tower 2. The janitorial staff often reported to Campbell that they would see a shadowy figure roaming around the hallways. There were evenings when some of the doors would open and close on their own. Campbell himself once heard the sound of footsteps approaching him when nobody else was present. Lights would also turn on and off and toilets would flush by themselves. On another occasion, late in the evening around 3:00 am, Campbell witnessed one of the elevator doors open, travel upward and then return to the same floor it had departed from. Campbell said it was as if someone or something was riding on the elevator. There had been no one else in Tower 2 at the time of that incident.

My good friend and parapsychological mentor, Darryll Walsh, use to work at the Halifax Shopping Centre when he was a teenager. It has been reported that an elevator repairman had fallen to his death one evening while working on the Tower 2 elevator. Besides the elevator travelling on its own accord without any passengers, the sounds of someone working inside the shaft were occasionally reported.

Campbell researched the history of 7001 Mumford Road which is where the Halifax Shopping Centre is currently situated. Campbell said that the property was mostly vacant land, but at one point in time had once contained boy's orphanage. This orphanage was the Saint Patrick's Boys Home. In 1956, the Timothy Eaton Company applied to the City of Halifax in order to have the land re-zoned for a shopping center. Construction on the Halifax Shopping Centre commenced in February 1961 with its grand opening being held on September 11, 1962.

Darryll Walsh said underneath all of the stores was a storage space made up of metal fencing which he nicknamed “the catacombs”. A young man who worked at the mall was said to have committed suicide in the catacombs. Mall employees have reported hearing the sounds of someone moving around one of the storage spaces or hearing the weeping sounds of a person.

Campbell confirmed that the Halifax Shopping Centre does indeed have tunnels that run underneath the stores which were used as storage space. Oddly enough, Campbell also said that there is a very strange staircase which doesn’t go anywhere. I don’t believe this strange stairwell has any supernatural meaning. It is most likely the remnants from one of the many facelifts the shopping centre has endured.

I spoke with another friend and security supervisor who believes he had an apparitional experience one evening. It was around 2:00 am one foggy maritime night in October. Harold Quinn was working a backshift alone at the Halifax Shopping Centre. He was monitoring the closed circuit television system when he noticed someone walking through the west lot between Sears Canada warehouse pick up and the Bowlarama. He saw a suspicious looking male wearing an older style black trench coat and a tall black top hat. He was walking toward Bayers Road. Security supervisor Quinn ran from the security office and jumped into the security patrol vehicle to investigate. He drove around the entire property looking for the suspicious male, but as quickly as he had appeared, he seemingly disappeared.

Security supervisor Quinn said he found Tower 1 creepier than Tower 2. While working another backshift one evening, he was in the 20 Vic Property Management Company board room watching television. The sound of footsteps caught his attention. He got up from his chair and looked outside, but there was nobody there.

Security supervisor Quinn advised that there have been many deaths which have occurred at Halifax Shopping Centre. He corroborated the fact that someone did die in Tower 2 and that the mall elevators would often operate on their own accord during the evening hours in the absence of human intervention.

The Halifax Shopping Centre certainly has all of the makings for a haunting. You've heard the facts from two credible witnesses and a parapsychologist. It is time for the jury to deliberate and reach a verdict. Haunted or not haunted? You decide.

THE USS CHESAPEAKE

Point Pleasant Park is located at 5530 Point Pleasant Drive in the south end of the Halifax peninsula. Halifax Regional Municipality rents the site from the British Government for 1 shilling a year with a 999 year lease. The 75 hectare area is only open to the public up until midnight.

Security Officer Paul Campbell used to volunteer with the Halifax Regional Police Service in the early 2000's. He was told by two Halifax police Sergeants, whom I personally know and have worked with, that they had seen some strange things in the park while on patrol. Police officers reported seeing fires and other strange things in the woods at Point Pleasant Park, but upon investigation there would be nothing there.

The park contains the ruins of several forts and has historical significance relating to the War of 1812 between Canada and the United States of America. There was a battle between the *HMS Shannon* and the *USS Chesapeake* in Boston Harbour. The crew from the *USS Chesapeake* were taken prisoner and brought to Halifax, Nova Scotia. The ship itself was repaired and taken into service by the Royal Navy. Witnesses have reported seeing the ghost ship of the *USS Chesapeake* sailing off of the coast of Point Pleasant Park under the full moon's light during hot June nights.

HALIFAX PROVINCIAL COURT

Sheriff Kent Kone is a 15 year veteran with the Nova Scotia Sheriff Services. He is very familiar with the history of the Halifax Provincial Court situated at 5250 Spring Garden Road, having been posted there for six years.

Sheriff Kone said that there is at least one ghost who resides at the courthouse. The staff have nick named this entity "Bill". Bill frequently resides in the courthouse attic. A custodian, who has since passed on, once saw an apparition materialize in the attic. Sheriff Kone explained that the attic is one of the only original pieces of the court house which was constructed during the 1850's. The attic acted as a make shift accommodation for a caretaker at one point during its history. Sheriff Kone advised that the last hanging happened in 1935 at the back of the courthouse which is now a staff parking lot. Local folklore amongst the courthouse personnel states that at the end of the hanging, the wood from the gallows was used for upkeep purposes in the attic. Sheriff Kone has seen beams of wood in the attic with notches cut into them. He believes that it is possible wood from hanging had been used for renovations because back then, people didn't waste anything.

Sheriff Kone said during renovations of the courthouse, it is not uncommon to find old leather shoes hidden throughout. The leather shoes were hidden throughout the courthouse to ward off spirits. Some of the floor joists in the attic still have leather shoes embedded in them.

Thanks to archaeologists, we know that since at least the

early modern period between 1,500 A.D and 1,800 A.D., humans have been hiding objects in the structure of buildings to ward off evil influences such as demons, ghosts and witches. Shoes are the most commonly discovered items; however, written charms, dried cats, horse skulls, and witch bottles have also been used. Chimneys, under floors, above ceilings, around doors and woods and in roof tops are common hiding places.

This historic tradition is based on folklore in which many people believed that witches were attracted to the human scent of a shoe. It was believed that once the witch entered the shoe, they would find themselves trapped. Archaeologists also attribute this tradition to a legend involving a non-canonised saint named Sir John Schorne who was said to have once captured the Devil himself in a boot. Nonetheless, this tradition still continues today. I have investigated several alleged haunted houses in which the home owners have buried or hidden religious medallions and objects throughout their home and property.

He has worked several backshifts and even though he rationally knows that an old building such as the courthouse is prone to drafty windows and strange settling noises, he can't help but acknowledge the powerful and uncomfortable feeling that overcomes him when he is in the attic. It is not just Sheriff Kone who feels this way. None of the courthouse staff like attending the attic. In fact, there is a ritual to announce yourself with a "hello" before entering the attic. Sheriff Kone was trained to do this in an attempt to appease any spirits who may be lurking in the attic.

There are also original cells which are non-operational and

dirt flooring in an old wing of the courthouse which is not used. There are strange markings on the wall which have never been explained.

Underneath the grand staircase in the front lobby of the courthouse lies the modern day cell block. You can access it through the security door. One evening after night court, Sheriff Kone, two other Sheriff's and two cleaners were divvying up their final tasks for the evening to make sure that no one was hiding in the courthouse before securing the doors. No one was jumping at the opportunity to check the attic due to the stories about the ghost. Sheriff Kone quickly jumped on the task of checking the modern day cell block, thinking that he may avoid any unusual encounters with Bill the ghost.

Sheriff Kone went to the secure door near the grand staircase and swiped his security card. He turned the door knob and opened the door. As the door opened about a foot and a half, someone grabbed the door handle from the other side and slammed it shut. Sheriff Kone let go of the door knob and starred at it for a couple of seconds. He quickly used his card again and opened the door. He looked behind the door but there was no there. He began rationalizing what had just happened. He knew that it wasn't the other two sheriffs or the two cleaners because he had just seen them depart for their duties about 90 seconds prior. There was no draft and nobody located down the long stretch of hallway behind the secure door. To this day, Sheriff Kone still gets shivers throughout his body whenever he recalls the incident.

Several years ago, parapsychologist Dr. Darryll Wash spoke

to staff at the courthouse while researching stories for his book *Ghosts of Nova Scotia.* The staff told him that they can sometimes hear the sounds of someone moving around in the attic. He was also told that a custodian had quit after seeing a pair of eyes peering at him from within the darkness of the attic.

I spoke to another Sheriff friend of mine, Carl Murphy who also worked at the Halifax Provincial Court. While working night court, Sheriff Murphy was monitoring the cameras when something caught his attention. The chandelier in the main foyer began to sway back and forth on its own accord. Sheriff Murphy was the only sheriff working at the time and said that the building didn't have any ventilation systems or heat pumps and all of the doors and windows were closed.

Sheriff Murphy corroborated Sheriff Kone's testimony regarding pieces of the gallows being located in the attic. Sheriff Murphy was more fascinated with the local lore that a tunnel runs from the Halifax Provincial Court House underneath the Halifax Old Burial Grounds all the way to the Nova Scotia Lieutenant Governor's house situated on Barrington Street. He has never seen the tunnel himself, but he is convinced that there is a passage way contained within the Halifax Provincial Court building. The City of Halifax is known for its secret tunnels. The famous Halifax brew master Alexander Keith had a tunnel which led from his brewery located on Lower Water Street to his residence a couple of blocks away on Hollis Street.

HALIFAX SUPREME COURT FAMILY DIVISION

The Supreme Court Family Division building is located at 3380 Devonshire Avenue in Halifax, Nova Scotia. The building used to be the old Richmond School house. On December 6, 1917 the French munitions ship *Mont Blanc* collided with the *Imo* causing the devastating Halifax explosion. Over 2,000 Haligonians were killed during the catastrophe, including 500 children. Some of the deceased children were students looking out the window toward the Halifax harbour before the massive explosion rocked the city. The building is said to be haunted by the spirit of one of the deceased students, a little girl named Annie Campbell.

One evening, Sheriff Carl Murphy was working a parent information session, at the Supreme Court Family Division. It is a mandatory training session for parents going through a divorce. The classroom is located on the lower level of the court house.

While class was in session, Sheriff Murphy was sitting on the main level of the courthouse observing the upstairs cameras. He said it wasn't quite dark outside because he recalled seeing the evening sunset beaming through the windows. There was no court in session at the time and nobody should have been upstairs. While he was monitoring the camera, he suddenly saw the apparition of what he believed to be Annie standing in the sunlight. She was standing still and appeared to be staring at something in the hallway.

Sheriff Murphy said that she is known to frequent the courthouse. She is often heard running and giggling throughout the corridors with the sound of other children. When she runs up the old wooden steps they audibly creek. Sheriff Murphy said the activity doesn't frighten him, but some of the other sheriff's don't like the supernatural activity.

THE ST. CATHERINES POLTERGEIST

On February 6, 1970 Niagara Regional Police Constable Bob Crawford responded to a domestic disturbance call at apartment three situated at 237 Church Street in St. Catherines, Ontario. Once his investigation was complete, he exited the apartment but was approached by another female named Barbara Paige who said she was the occupant of apartment one. Mrs. Paige told Cst. Crawford that she needed help in her apartment.

As Cst. Crawford entered her apartment, he observed that the dwelling unit was in total disarray with kitchen drawers pulled out and tossed onto the floor. Mrs. Paige lived in the apartment with her husband John and their two sons. She told Cst. Crawford that objects and furniture began spontaneously moving on their own approximately 10 days previous. Cst. Crawford noted in his investigative report that after listening to the story, he began "thinking both she and her husband were mental." Suddenly, a Roman Catholic priest named Father Stevens arrived at the apartment. Father Stevens told Cst. Crawford that he was aware of the disturbances and had been assisting the family. Father Stevens said that he had witnessed a bed being pulled away from a wall on its own accord. When Father Stevens placed the bed back in its proper place, it would pull away from the wall again.

Cst. Crawford moved everyone in the apartment into the living room. Prior to Cst. Crawford leaving the kitchen, he moved a chair out of his way and placed it against the kitchen table. Father Stevens heard the sounds of footsteps walking from the living room into the kitchen. Cst. Crawford and Father Stevens went into the kitchen and the chair that Cst. Crawford had moved was now located in the middle of the kitchen several feet away from where he had positioned it. Cst. Crawford left the residence as Father Stevens was present to assist the family.

On February 7, 1970 at 10:00 pm, Cst. Crawford was dispatched to 237 Church Street to investigate another domestic disturbance at unit number three. While interviewing witness Mrs. Baines, Cst. Crawford noticed that she appeared visibly shaken. He asked her what was wrong in which she told Cst. Crawford that she had just witnessed a bed in apartment one lift up off the floor with no support. She was sober and appeared to be a reasonable person so Cst. Crawford said he had to see this activity for himself.

Cst. Crawford attended apartment one and spoke to John and Barbara Paige whom he had just met the previous day. They showed Cst. Crawford the bed. In his investigative report, he wrote that the bed was "2 feet off the floor at one end and was unsupported". Cst. Crawford couldn't believe his eyes, so he went to go get Cst. Colledge who was standing outside the apartment. When they returned, the bed was in the same position but it was now supported by two chairs which had materialized.

There were two other ladies present at the time. Mrs. McKinnon and the landlord's daughter. Mrs. McKinnon told Cst. Crawford that earlier in the day around 11:00 am, she was in apartment one when she observed a heavy rocking chair fly from one side of the room to the other and tip over on its back without making too much sound. Suddenly, Cst. Crawford heard a knocking and the sound of an object landing in the children's room. The Paige's older 11 year old son, Peter, was awakened as Cst. Crawford entered the room and turned on the bedroom light. Cst. Crawford saw a doll which he had previously seen hanging on one wall approximately six feet from the bed. It was now lying beside Peter. Cst. Crawford told Peter to wake up his younger brother and go into his mother's bedroom. Constable Mike McMenanin and Constable Bill Weir arrived on scene along with friends of the family, Mr. and Mrs. Asher. Cst. Crawford had everyone move into the living room.

Cst. Crawford explained what was happening to Cst. Weir. Cst. Weir told Cst. Crawford that on January 15 he and Constable Batorski had responded to strange noises and occurrences reported by tenants of a different unit number at 237 Church Street. Cst. Weir said he had contacted the St. Catherines Engineering Department who inspected the apartment building but did not find any structural issues. The utility companies were also called in to inspect their services, all of which were operating normally.

Cst. Crawford saw the children lying on the bed in their parent's bedroom when suddenly he saw a picture fall from the wall and land on Peter's head. A minute or so later, a table lamp in the bedroom fell over and a large heavy chest of drawers moved from the wall and back again. A chair in the opposite corner of the room also levitated in the air and slammed forcefully down to the floor. The events were witnessed by everyone present. Cst. Crawford also saw objects on a dressing table in the other part of the room hurled to the floor with the exception of an alarm clock which moved in the opposite direction and landed by Peter on the far side of the bed. Cst.

Crawford made note that there was no vibration of the doors or other parts of the room and objects on the wall remained undisturbed. Cst. Crawford told John to bring the children somewhere else for the evening as it wasn't safe for them to remain in the apartment.

Cst. Weir witnessed bowling trophies being tossed off the shelf one at a time. He also witnessed the kitchen wall clock unplug itself and land on the floor without making any noise. The activity appeared to be surrounding Peter. Cst. Crawford said when Peter would walk by the pictures on the wall, they would sway "in the same manner as a dog wags its tail when it is happy to see its master." The witnesses saw an unseen force push Peter against the wall on several occasions. Cst. Weir wrote in his occurrence report that he had seen Peter thrown at least a dozen times for no apparent reason.

On one occasion, Peter was sitting in a large, heavy chair when it flipped over on its own and pinned Peter to the ground. Two police officers had to lift the chair off of Peter. On another occasion, Peter was sitting on the lap of one of the police officers when something tried to remove him. It took the strength of two officers to keep Peter from moving off of the officer's lap.

Officers also witnessed a sofa couch with four people sitting on it levitate approximately eighteen inches off the floor. Cst. Weir and Cst. Crawford said it seemed like the only two items which weren't affected was a crucifix and a picture of the Immaculate Virgin Mary.

As the children were getting dressed in the living room, a book case between the wall and Mr. Asher tipped over for no apparent reason and fell to the floor. A senior priest from the Cathedral, Monsignor Delaney, arrived to stay with the mother and Mr. and Mrs. Asher.

On February 11, 1970 Cst. Weir, Cst. Crawford, Cst. McMenanin along with Detectives Richardson and Sandison attended apartment one again. There were also several civilian witnesses present including Dr. Coholan, Dr. Feitelsohn, the family lawyer Mr. McQuilken, Father Stevens, Father Delaney and of course John and Barbara Paige, Peter and his 8 year old brother. The lawyer was there to represent the family as there had been a leak at the Niagara Regional Police about the strange occurrences and the media was in a frenzy. Approximately 45 minutes into the investigation, Detective Richardson witnessed the chair that Peter was sitting in lift abruptly six inches off of the floor and slam down. The casters which were under the legs of the chair were now about four inches from the legs. Det. Richardson examined the chair and could not find any explanation for what he had witnessed. No other phenomena was witnessed at that time, but Det. Richardson received a call from Mr. McQuilken later that evening saying that some phenomena was taking place again. Det. Richardson did not attend the residence again but noted in his investigative report that the family did not want any media attention as they were concerned for Peter's wellbeing at school and their own wellbeing within the community. Constables Weir, Crawford and McMenanin said that when Peter wasn't present at the apartment, the activity ceased. According to Cst. Weir, the poltergeist activity lasted a total of 28 days.

This incident which occurred in St. Catherines, is a classic poltergeist case. Although the word poltergeist originates from the German words polter(n) which means to make noise knock rattle and geist which means ghost, poltergeist cases have nothing to do with ghosts. The poltergeist haunting phenomena has undergone a lot of changes since I first started studying and investigating the paranormal.

Classic parapsychological theories hypothesized that the haunting characteristics manifested by a poltergeist were the result of a ghost or energy emanating from a prepubescent teenager, usually a female. Contemporary parapsychology now suggests after decades of research that the poltergeist effects are caused by living people, known as Mind Matter Interaction (MMI), specifically Recurrent Spontaneous Psychokinesis (RSPK). RSPK in this sense, simply means paranormal activity such as the movement of objects spontaneously happening over a period of time which emulates a haunting. It can be manifested by one or more people living at a location, often, but not always, troubled adolescents. The events are believed to be intrinsically meaningful. Some parapsychologists believe that the poltergeist activity is a way of relieving one's stress through the physical expression of unconscious feelings.

Unlike a haunting which can continue for years, poltergeist activity has a short duration which usually lasts anywhere from a week and half up to a year and half. Although poltergeist activity has similarities to a haunting, there are some unique differences. The haunting activity ceases if the living agent is no longer present. Spontaneous fires or water appearing along with injuries to people are reported during poltergeist hauntings but are rare in apparitional hauntings. Apparitions are rarely seen during a poltergeist haunting and when they are, they do not appear humanlike but are often described as dark, distorted figures. Auditory voices in poltergeist hauntings are also extremely rare. Poltergeist cases usually involve actual items being moved, thrown or breaking whereas discarnate entity haunting field investigations often report the auditory sounds of items being moved or broken. Discarnate entity hauntings tend to be more hallucinatory in nature and do not correspond to actual physical disturbances unlike poltergeist hauntings.

SHAG HARBOUR UFO CRASH

Two hours and fifty minutes west of Halifax is the small fishing village of Shag Harbour. It has been called the Roswell of Canada because it is home to the Government of Canada's only documented UFO crash.

On the evening of October 4, 1967 there was a rash of UFO signings across the southern portion of Nova Scotia. A local fisherman named Laurie Wickens and four of his friends were travelling along the coast on Highway 3 in his vehicle. Laurie observed four or five peculiar looking lights that would flash in sequence starting from one end and continuing straight through to the other end flying in the sky. The lights appeared to be on a 45 degree angle and were descending. The lights disappeared and a loud crash echoed throughout the little fishing community. Laurie and his passengers pulled into a gravel parking lot near an Irish Moss plant and exited the vehicle. They could see the object in the water approximately 700 feet from the shoreline. They described pale yellow lights in the water attached to a darker object, possibly that of an airliner. The object was estimated to be 60 feet wide and 10 feet high and it was drifting with the ocean's tide.

Laurie went to find a pay phone and placed a call to the Barrington Royal Canadian Mounted Police. Corporal Victor Werbicki spoke to a very excited Laurie who reported a possible downed airliner. In disbelief, Corporal Werbicki asked Laurie if he had been drinking. All of a sudden, the detachment started receiving more calls from other locals reporting the same thing. An investigation commenced and local fishermen and RCMP officers began searching the waters for a downed airliner. They located a mysterious thick yellow sparkling foam on the water's surface. There was also the smell of sulphur and bubbles coming from the water toward the surface. After five hours of searching, no bodies, jet fuel, oil or wreckage had been located. The search continued on for days afterward by the RCMP, Canadian Coast Guard and Canadian Navy to no avail. The search produced no bodies or aircraft.

NELLIE VAUGHN

The town of Coventry, Rhode Island is located in Kent County and is home to approximately 35,000 people. It is policed by the Coventry Police Department.

On September 1, 2018 just before 12:00 am, the Coventry Police Department received a call for service advising that a woman wearing a white wedding dress had come out of the woods on Hopkins Hollow Road yelling for help. Officers Paul Rebello and Zachary Mason searched the area but did not locate anyone matching that description. The police department posted on their Facebook page that it may have been a restless spirit from the Hopkins Hollow Cemetery or the ghost of Nellie Vaughn who wondered from her resting place in the Plain Meeting House Cemetery to say that she is "perfectly pleasant and not a vampire." The Coventry Police Department asked if anyone had any information regarding the woman or apparition to telephone the police department, but no further calls were received.

On September 18, 2018 I attended the Plain Meeting House Cemetery also known as Rhode Island Historical Cemetery number two. This is the resting spot of Nellie Vaughn who died in 1889 at the age of 19. Her tombstone has since been stolen, but it use to read "I am waiting and watching for you." New England folklore states that Nellie was a vampire. Locals speculate that this is why the spirit of Nellie can't rest. Her spirit remains on this plain to set the record straight that she wasn't a vampire. Over the years, there have been many ghostly sightings of Nellie. She has been described as a young woman wearing Victorian style attire. She has been seen walking down the nearby roads or sitting near her grave.

My visit to the gravesite proved to be an interesting one. While traveling down Plain Meeting House Road, the wipers on the vehicle turned on all by themselves for three minutes. Upon arrival at the cemetery, they suddenly stopped. It was a dry day, without any rain or moisture.

I tried to locate Nellie Vaughn's final resting spot, but her tombstone is missing and it was very difficult to pin point her exact resting spot. Unlike suspected vampire Mercy Brown's tombstone located in Exeter, Rhode Island, no gifts or offerings were left for Nellie.

Locals have reported capturing strange phenomena in photographs and on audio recordings. Other witnesses have reported hearing a disembodied female voice saying "I am perfectly pleasant." Others have reported being touched, poked or being scratched. Other than the windshield wipers mysteriously turning on and off all by themselves, I did not witness anything further.

PREMONITION

Alright partner, let me do all the talking on this next call. We are going to explore a premonition involving a situation with an independent agency which investigates complaints of potential police wrongdoing. Professional standards, internal affairs or independent agency postings are always difficult for everyone involved. Professional standards and internal affairs are usually police officers investigating police officer's actions and independent agencies are usually a mixture of retired or seconded police officers and civilians investigating police officer's actions. The officers who work those units have a difficult job because they often are alienated and resented by their coworkers. Let's face it though, if you are receiving a call from them, it is most likely not to thank you for your service and tell you what a wonderful job you have been doing.

On June 27, 2018 I was at home on sick leave after having been diagnosed with post-traumatic stress disorder which arose as a result of my service with the Royal Canadian Mounted Police. I woke up around 10:00 am and sat up in bed for a minute as I was trying to get the energy to go upstairs and brew a coffee. Suddenly a vision or image of an ex-girlfriend that I had broken up with back in April appeared in my mind. It was a facial image of her. It only lasted for a couple of seconds and then it disappeared. As soon as the image disappeared an overwhelming feeling of despair came over me. As the feeling lingered, the following thought came into my mind "she made a malicious complaint against me with work." Suddenly the feelings and thought disappeared. I sat in bed for another minute thinking that it was very strange that those thoughts and feelings came over me as I had not been thinking about work or the ex-girlfriend whatsoever during my recovery at home.

Approximately twenty minutes later while I was sipping on my coffee, my cellular phone rang. I answered the call and an investigator from the Nova Scotia Serious Incident Response Team (SIRT) identified himself. I was told that someone had made a complaint against me. The investigator said that the file was concluded and that their head director agreed with the investigative findings that the complaint had no merit to it. The investigator then told me that he wanted to meet with me in person to discuss the allegation and who had made the complaint. Although I agreed to meet with the investigator, I did not need him to tell me who had made the complaint, because I already knew. As soon as I answered the phone call and heard that it was a SIRT investigator, I knew that the ex-girlfriend had made a complaint against me. This event is known in parapsychology as a premonition.

Premonitions are defined as a feeling or impression that something is about to happen, especially something ominous or dire, yet about which no normal information is available. The word itself stems from the Latin words prae meaning "prior to" and monitio meaning "warning". As a parapsychological investigator, it is extremely difficult to investigate and collect data on premonition cases because they are spontaneous in nature. In fact premonitions actual defy the known logical principal of antecedence (causality) which means that an effect does not happen before its cause.

I do believe that certain individuals possess and know how to utilize their psychical abilities, but I am not one of them. I am not sure why I had this spontaneous premonition, however, as you have just read, it couldn't have been more accurate and manifested within a matter of hours.

THE BRIDGEPORT CONNECTICUT POLTERGEIST

In late 1974 there was a media frenzy underway surrounding a haunted house in the city of Bridgeport, Connecticut. The house was situated at 966 Lindley Street and was inhabited by Gerald and Laura Goodin, along with their adopted daughter Marcia. Due to the extensive media coverage, the field investigation attracted the attention of many witnesses, some of which included police officers from the Bridgeport Police Department. The Bridgeport Police Department had recorded several eye witness interviews during the haunting. Famous demonologists Ed and Lorraine Warren who were residing in Munroe, Connecticut also became aware of the occurrence and offered their assistance.

1972 was the first time that the Bridgeport Police Department became aware of the Lindley Street haunting after the Goodin family made their first police report regarding the strange occurrences. The Goodins described classic haunting characteristics such as pounding noises, seeing a partial apparition, doors opening and closing and furniture being moved on their own. They reported the incident to the police hoping that they could determine the cause of the pounding and other phenomena occurring, but they were unable to provide an explanation.

One evening on November 22, 1974 the Goodins were experiencing a barrage of psychokinetic activity including large pieces of furniture being moved on their own and levitating, items on the wall being removed and smashed and a television moving on its own accord. Bridgeport Police Department were dispatched to an “unknown help call” at 966 Lindley Street. Once on scene, several police officers witnessed a refrigerator move and levitate across the floor. Other police officers witnessed a television levitate in the air and rotate clockwise while floating. One police officer’s observations depicted a scene that looked like a break and enter suspect had ransacked each room leaving open drawers and personal possessions strewn about the residence.

Bridgeport Police Department records document several unusual events which occurred inside the Goodin home. Amongst the anomalous phenomena was a crucifix which had exploded from a wall in front of witnesses. The Goodin’s cat Sam, made noises that sounded like it was speaking English words, the sounds of loud pounding on the walls and in one such instance a lounge chair in which Marcia was sitting in moved rapidly backwards and flipped over.

A few weeks into the police and parapsychological investigation, Marcia was caught by a Bridgeport police officer trying to tip over a television with her foot when she thought no one was looking. After being confronted about what the police officer witnessed, Marcia took responsibility for all of the activities in the house. Bridgeport Police Department Superintendent Joseph Walsh declared the Linley Street haunting a hoax and concluded their official investigation, despite paranormal activity still occurring for several more weeks. Some say that this was a tactic by the Bridgeport Police Department in order to help disperse the large crowd of curious bystanders and media outlet personnel. Unofficially, the Bridgeport Police Department continued to assist the Goodin family with the phenomena. A Bridgeport Police Department Captain also ordered some officers to assist in the Psychical Research Foundation and Spiritual Frontiers Fellowship's parapsychological investigation. Eventually all of the activity did cease.

The Bridgeport, Connecticut haunting is another classic poltergeist case. All of the aforementioned events are classic poltergeist haunting characteristics. The only rare occurrence was witnesses seeing the apparitional hand, which isn't unheard of but is uncommon in poltergeist cases.

So who was the living agent causing the disturbances in this case? The parapsychological investigation wasn't clearly able to determine whether it was Laura, Marcia or both who were creating the manifestations. Laura was an overbearing, destructive and over protective mother. It was no wonder she was. She had suffered the dreaded mother's worst nightmare as her 6 year old son had been stricken with cerebral palsy and died in 1967 at the age of 6. After their son's death, Gerald and Laura decided to adopt Marcia.

The other side of the parapsychological investigation looked at Marcia being the living agent responsible for manifesting the activity. Due to Marcia's indigenous background, she had olive colored skin and was picked on at school. The bullying became so bad that at one point she had been beaten so severely that she had to be put into a full body brace. Gerald and Laura withdrew Marcia out of public school and began home schooling her. The frustration, loneliness and stress that Marcia was feeling is a perfect recipe for poltergeist activity to manifest. However, the tragic grief from her son's death on top of the newly added stress of Marcia being bullied is also a perfect recipe for poltergeist activity.

Having two living agents suffering as much as Laura and Marcia together in the same household has also been known to manifest a poltergeist haunting. This is why parapsychological investigators were unable to determine who or what was responsible for the Bridgeport, Connecticut poltergeist haunting.

THE ESPANOLA APPARITION

On September 20, 2014 police detective Solomon Romero was working an evening shift at the Espanola Police Department. As he looked up at the surveillance cameras, he observed a transparent human shaped apparitional figure walk through the ear parking lot. This is an area of the police station which is locked and secure from public access.

The surveillance footage is quite blurry; however, it does show what appears to be legs moving in normal sequential order as if someone was walking. The apparition walked through a chain linked fence. Espanola Police made statements to the media that there would be no way a person could enter the area without opening the gates which would trigger their alarm system.

Other police officers with the Espanola Police Department believe that the building is haunted because some have seen and heard the ghost. Detective Romero said that some officers have felt breathing on the back of their neck while working in the briefing room.

The identity of the Espanola Police Department's ghost remains unknown. The cliché of the police station being built on ancient burial grounds has been ruled out. Officers also attest that no one has ever died in the building. It appears as though this haunting investigation has gone cold and remains as one of Espanola Police's unsolved cases.

THE CANADIAN X-FILES

This next story is something straight out of the television show *The X-Files* partner, so keep an open mind on what you are about to read. A UFO researcher asked to meet with me at a downtown Halifax coffee shop. During the meeting, I received information from the UFO researcher that is of little known fact unless you are involved in the study of Unidentified Flying Objects. I was told that the Royal Canadian Mounted Police used to document UFO sightings and would forward them to Saint Mary's University professor and Reverend Michael Walter Burke-Gaffney for further investigation and analysis. The UFO researcher also told me that the RCMP files are held in the Saint Mary's University archives and that where I was a student at Saint Mary's University, I would have access to view and copy the documents from the library. Like my favourite character *Fox Mulder*, I was on a qucst to locate this new and exciting information.

I attended the Saint Mary's University library and requested to see the Burke-Gaffney files, particularly anything having to do with his UFO research. The university provided me with a folder containing 210 pages of RCMP police reports, memorandums, hand written notes, newspaper articles on UFOs from around the world and letters written by citizens containing their UFO experiences. Some of the police file numbers end with an "X" for all intents and purposes, making these cases X-Files.

Father Burke-Gaffney was certainly an interesting gentleman. He earned his Bachelors of Engineering in 1917 from Dublin National University and served in the Air Ministry from

1918-1920. He moved to Canada and became an ordained priest in 1930. He earned a Master's degree at Georgetown University in Washington before completing his Doctorate of Astronomy in 1935. During his own time, Father Burke-Gaffney conducted extensive research on many subjects including UFOs, superstition and demonology. He passed away on January 14, 1979 in Halifax, Nova Scotia.

The fact that Father Burke-Gaffney assisted the Canadian Government with their UFO investigations is both intriguing and extraordinary. Certainly he had the credentials to provide astronomical explanations for these events. However, a Roman Catholic priest stepping outside his religious realm to investigate a phenomena associated to the potential for extraterrestrial life to exist is uncommon. The UFO phenomena doesn't coincide with Catholic beliefs, making this event extraordinary.

The following two UFO investigations are from Father Burke-Gaffney's collection. The first UFO sighting was witnessed by a former Royal Canadian Air Force pilot. The second investigation is a close encounter of the second kind in which a UFO causes a physical effect. Were these police investigations simply astronomical events? Secret and experimental military aircraft? Or is it possible that we are being visited by intelligent extraterrestrial life forms? I'll leave it in your capable hands to decide, partner.

COLCHESTER COUNTY UFO SIGHTING

According to Father Burke-Gaffney's records in RCMP file number

67-400-43, in the late summer and early fall of 1967, there was a rash of Unidentified Flying Object sightings in the Colchester County area of Nova Scotia. One of the more interesting UFO sightings occurred on October 12, 1967 shortly after 9:00 pm. Dr. N. Budgey of Truro noticed an object of some kind in the sky north of his position, but he couldn't estimate the distance or height. Dr. Budgey described the object moving slowly in a southward manner and emanating a yellow or orange light. The sighting lasted approximately 10 minutes and its appearance was of a cluster of reddish coloured lights. The object suddenly disappeared. Dr. Budgey was a former Royal Canadian Air Force pilot who was part of the Faculty of the Nova Scotia Teacher's College. He was a well-respected, responsible and reliable community member. At first, he was of the opinion that it was one of the constellations, but due to its movement he came to the conclusion that it must have been some kind of craft, possibly a helicopter. However, Dr. Budgey contacted the Canadian Forces Basc in Debert, Nova Scotia and was advised that there was no such aircraft known to be in the area at the time. Given that information, Dr. Budgey felt that it was important to report the matter to the RCMP.

OROMOCTO, NEW BRUNSWICK UFO SIGHTING

On March 13, 1973 in Oromocto, New Brunswick RCMP file number 73-400-2 tells Ms. Marilyn Abbott's reported UFO encounter. According to Father Burke-Gaffney's records, Ms.

Abbott was traveling alone on Waasis Road from Highway number 7 around 11:40 pm. Ms. Abbott noticed an object appear in the clear night sky that was shaped like the moon and was the size of a vehicle. She described the object as being a bright non-fluorescent white with a white halo light about the exterior of the object. There was no sound emanating from the object. When she noticed the object was coming closer to her, she increased her car speed to approximately 50 to 60 miles per hour. Once the object was completely overhead, Ms. Abbott's vehicle stalled out and would not re start. Her headlights also went out. She was driving a standard shift vehicle but was adamant her vehicle would not start. She jumped out of her car and ran to a nearby home for help. After running approximately 50 yards, she turned back to look at her car and noticed the object was gone. The car lights were turned back on. Ms. Abbott made it to the Bulger residence. Fearing that they may not believe her story, she neglected to tell them about her UFO encounter but asked if she could use the telephone to call her father. Her father attended the Bulger residence and picked her up. They drove directly to the Oromocto Town RCMP Detachment to report the incident. Ms. Abbott was quite distraught and the police recommended she attend the Oromocto Hospital for a sedative and they would follow up with her the following day.

The following day, Cpl K. H. Latchford attended the scene with Ms. Abbott and her father. Ms. Abbot showed Cpl. Latchford where her vehicle had stopped, but there was nothing else located at the scene. Cpl. Latchford interviewed Mr. Camille Bulger who advised he was home when Ms. Abbott attended his house. Mr.

Bulger said after Ms. Abbott's father was called, he accompanied her back to her vehicle. Mr. Bulger said the vehicle was found running and the head lights were on.

Cpl. Latchford contacted the control tower at Fredericton Airport and was advised that they had scheduled flights depart the airport at 11:00 pm and again at 12:20 am that evening. Cpl. Latchford contacted Canadian Forces Base in Gagetown and was advised that there were no helicopters in the air after 11:00 pm that evening.

Cpl. Latchford could not locate any other witnesses to the events and felt he had exhausted all of his investigative avenues. He even questioned Ms. Abbott on the possible use of drugs, however, she had never been involved in their usage. Cpl. Latchford even followed up with Oromocto Hospital who advised him that she showed no effects from the use of drugs. The UFO sighting remained explained.

RECORD GROUP 18 - ROYAL CANADIAN MOUNTED POLICE CANADIAN X-FILES

The Library and Archives Canada contains Canadian government records pertaining to Unidentified Flying Objects. With respect to the Royal Canadian Mounted Police, these files are recorded under Record Group 18 which contains UFO sightings from 1959 to 1987 inclusive. Through the Access to Information and Privacy Act, these RCMP files were obtained.

GRAND FALLS, NEWFOUNDLAND UFO SIGHTING

On December 28, 1968 in the town of Grand Falls, Newfoundland four RCMP officers witnessed an unidentified flying object. At approximately 7:55 pm, Cpl. E. L. Hawboldt of the Grand Falls Highway Patrol was travelling west on the Trans-Canada Highway near Jumper's Brook. He saw a bright white light, tinged with amber which appeared to be at an altitude of approximately 1000 feet. The light was flickering and pulsating slowly and was travelling in a westerly direction. At first, Cpl. Hawboldt thought it may have been a helicopter.

At approximately 8:00 pm, Cpl. Hawboldt notified the other RCMP officers in the area of his sighting. Cst. A. F. Hatchette of the Grand Falls Highway Patrol was travelling on the Trans-Canada Highway near Bishop's Falls. Cst. Hatchette acknowledged that he had seen a similar described object at 7:30 pm travelling in a westerly direction over Exploits Bay. Cst. Hatchette proceeded to travel west on the Trans-Canada Highway and was able to observe the object that Cpl. Hawboldt reported. Cst. T. G. Chamberlain was with Cst. W. S. King in Bishop's Falls when he heard Cpl. Hawboldt's report. Cst. Chamberlain saw a flickering, bright white light, tinged with amber in the sky to the northwest. The light appeared to be a couple of miles west of Bishop's Falls still travelling in a northwest direction. Cst. Chamberlain pointed the object out to Cst. King. Both Constables could not hear any sounds emanating from the object nor could they hear the normal sound of any aircraft.

Cpl. Hawboldt and Cst. Hatchette followed the light to Grand Falls and watched it disappear to the northwest. Cst. Chamberlain and Cst. King went to a point just east of the western access road to Bishop's Falls on the Trans-Canada Highway and observed the light until it disappeared over the horizon. The light was lost from sight at approximately 8:10 pm.

On January 16, the RCMP sent the UFO report to Father Burke-Gaffney at Saint Mary's University On January 30, while talking about the UFO sighting at the Grand Falls RCMP Detachment, the local stenographer advised that she had seen a similar object pass over Bishop's Falls on several occasions during the month of December 1968. She stated it had been travelling in approximately the same westerly direction between 7:00 pm and 8:00 pm. There was no official explanation provided for this sighting in the RCMP file number 69-400-2.

CLARENVILLE, NEWFOUNDLAND UFO SIGHTING

On October 12, 1978 at 3:00 am, Chester Lethbridge and his wife reported a UFO sighting in the area of Random Island, Trinity Bay, Newfoundland. They watched the object for approximately two hours with the aid of binoculars from outside their residence. The sky was clear and they estimated the object to be at an altitude of approximately 500 feet. The object was circular in shape and approximately 35 to 40 feet in diameter. It flashed blue, red and yellow. Mrs. Lethbridge reported the incident to the Department of National Defence in Gander, Newfoundland.

Again on October 26, 1978 at 1:45 am, Mr. and Mrs. Lethbridge reported another UFO sighting; however, this time RCMP Constable Jim Blackwood who was posted to the Clarenville RCMP Detachment would attend the call for service. When he received the call, he couldn't see the object in the sky. He travelled to Marine Drive where he met Mr. and Mrs. Lethbridge about a half mile from Clarenville.

Cst. Blackwood saw the object traveling from West to East in the night sky. The sky was clear at the time. His first impression was that the object was a jet flying overhead. The object was observed at an estimated altitude of two to three thousand feet. Mr. Lethbridge passed Cst. Blackwood his binoculars and he saw the object was flashing blue. Cst. Blackwood decided to return to the RCMP Detachment and retrieve a telescope.

When Cst. Blackwood returned, the object was still in the sky, however, it was now stationary hovering over the Northeast coast of Random Island. Cst. Blackwood set the telescope up on its tripod and observed it at 15x magnification. He described the object as having rapid blue flashing lights on each side and one rapid flashing red and white light located on the top middle portion of the object. The undercarriage of the object was illuminated by some sort of light as well. The object was oval in shape with a large triangular shaped fin on the top that was flashing blue. The object was a dull metal color with no markings on it.

The object remained stationary in the sky for about one and a half hours before it began moving side to side prior to departing the Clarenville area. Cst. Blackwood estimated its rate of speed as being equivalent to a regular jet. The object continued moving until it disappeared from Cst. Blackwood's sight in the night's sky.

Before making an official report, Cst. Blackwood also checked out the brightest star in the sky with the telescope and he was completely sure that the object he and the Lethbridge's had seen was not a star. He was also positive that it was not a helicopter because at the magnification he was viewing the object; he would have seen rotor blades. Furthermore, he was convinced that it wasn't a conventional aircraft based on its movements and the lights. Cst. Blackwood stated that a normal aircraft has a red light above and below the fuselage but they are only activated during takeoff and landing. The incident was also reported to the Department of National Defence office in Gander, Newfoundland.

The 1978 Clarenville sighting is one that Cst. Blackwood will never forget. I had the opportunity to interview him over the telephone on November 1, 2019 about this sighting. He said the sighting completely changed his outlook on the UFO phenomena. He had been a non-believer in UFOs until this sighting. To this day he still can't say what kind of vehicle or aircraft he had seen that night.

The official government explanation for this sighting was noted as "most likely the planet Jupiter, which is quite brilliant. It rises about midnight in mid-October, and is near the meridian at sunrise. Saturn and several bright stars are also in the eastern sky at this time."

Cst. Blackwood assured me that the government's official explanation that the UFO was either the planet Jupiter or Saturn is simply not true. He advised me that A. G. McNamara who wrote the report never even review the case file or interviewed any of the witnesses. He also said that the UFO sighting occurred around the same time that Government of Canada did not like to publicly discuss the UFO phenomena. The only reason he gave two media interviews in uniform regarding the sighting was because the press had caught wind of the sighting and put pressure on the RCMP for a statement. Cst. Blackwood was ordered by superiors to speak to the media about it despite his apprehension and reluctance.

SPRINGHILL, NOVA SCOTIA UFO SIGHTING

On August 21, 1968 a husband, wife and their babysitter whose names are all redacted in the police report reported their UFO encounter to the Hamilton, Ontario RCMP Detachment in file 68-400-149 (Ham). They were returning to Hamilton, Ontario from Truro, Nova Scotia when they encountered 5 to 7 unidentified flying objects.

The UFO sighting occurred on August 15, 1968 at approximately 11:30 pm. The husband, wife and their babysitter were driving east on Highway 4 near Springhill, Nova Scotia. The husband provided a statement to RCMP Sgt. R. I. Evans. The husband reported that he was about 5 minutes north of River Philip. Suddenly, he noticed to the right of him was a group of some type of unconventional aircraft hovering at approximately 100 feet over the trees. To his left, he could see another craft approaching at a tremendous speed from about 5-6 miles away at an angle of sight about 25 to 30 degrees. The husband stated when he came to the centre of the activity; one of the crafts broke away from the group and moved over the highway in front of him. It began a slow descent of about 60 degrees. He was sure they were on a collision course. He slowed to a crawl but was terrified to stop the vehicle. He turned the radio off and put his head out the window but he couldn't hear any sounds. He noted a distinct outline of his vehicle was obscured by the series of rapidly and brilliantly flashing lights on the craft. The lights were extremely unconventional unlike any he had ever seen. When the closing craft was about 40-50 feet away at an estimated height of 35-40 feet above the ground, it suddenly veered up and disappeared in the distance behind him. The other group of UFOs to his right were still visible in his mirrors until he was too far away to see them any longer.

The husband said he had served three years in the Royal Canadian Navy and advised that 50% of his job was identifying objects from the lookout position. He stated that he had never seen anything like this before, and he was terrified when one of the objects came so close to his vehicle. He advised that he did not discuss the event with the other occupants of the vehicle because he didn't want to upset them. He also didn't want to mention the sighting to anyone for fear that people would think he was crazy. However, after discussing it with his wife and the baby sitter, they all felt that it should be reported to the authorities.

The wife provided a statement to Sgt. R. I Evans. In her statement, she said that her first reaction to seeing the aircraft was that they must be spraying a fire because they were so low, so numerous and so well lit up. But they travelled in such close proximity that she couldn't understand how they didn't collide. They appeared to be yellow and green lights and she counted at least 5 objects before one suddenly appeared over their vehicle. She was positive that the object was going to land and collide with them. She was too freighted to scream, but she prayed. The object reared up just in time to pass over them. She watched the object out her window which was to the right of the vehicle. She said the object was dark in colour with what looked like white dots all over it. It reminded her of the World War II planes on display in front of the CNE grounds. After they reached the end of the straight stretch of highway and rounded a corner, they lost sight of the craft since they were flying so low.

Finally the babysitter provided a statement to Sgt. R. I. Evans. In her statement, the babysitter said she saw 5 or 6 objects in which she thought were airplanes hovering just above the trees, maybe 50 feet or so. It was too dark to see the color of the planes and she recalled there were a lot of lights. She remembered a yellow one and it appeared at the front and was bigger than the rest. She said they slowed down and one passed in front of them which is the one they all thought was going to strike the vehicle. They didn't stop and didn't hear any sounds from the objects. She thought they were airplanes but she wasn't paying too much attention to them. She could only recall the yellow light. When she first glanced at the first object, she thought it was a flying saucer but then she thought she could see wings without lights so she didn't think anything more about it. The wife had asked the babysitter what she thought the objects were. The babysitter told the wife that she thought they were planes checking for a forest fire.

A small transcription of a statement taken from the babysitter by Sgt. R. I. Evans reads as follows;

Q. Do you think they were flying saucers?

A. I don't know. It seems funny there were so many and yet we couldn't hear them.

Q. Could they have been helicopters?

A. I don't think so. The window was open and we couldn't hear them. Helicopters make a lot of noise and these were real close.

Q. How many do you think there were all together?

A. There were 5 or 6.

Q. How long did you see them?

A. Between 5 and 10 minutes. We could see them for quite a ways before passing under. I did not look back.

Q. Were you scared of them?

A. No. Not until Toronto when we started talking about

them.

The police report concludes that all three witnesses were intelligent people and fully discussed the matter. No concerns about any of the witness's credibility were noted.

INUVIK, NORTHWEST TERRITORIES UFO SIGHTING

On January 20, 1967 at 1:25 am, RCMP Cst. A. Ford was patrolling the town of Inuvik, Northwest Territories when he noticed a flashing light moving through the sky from northeast to southwest. The object was moving toward the Mackenzie River. Cst. Ford described the light as resembling that of an aircraft coming in for a landing, but at the hour, it would have been unusual. He radioed his two partners at the detachment, Cst. St-Jean and Cst. Kaminski to notify them of the situation.

The light Cst. Ford observed was continuously flashing four different colors: red, green, blue and white. The flashes were similar to that of night flying aircraft, except that the variety of colours was not consistent with aircraft lights. He followed the light which led him to the road behind the W.C.P.C. building which was on a road that ran parallel to the river. He couldn't determine how far the light was because he couldn't make out any shape. It was quite apparent that the light was moving though.

Cst. Ford returned to the detachment to grab a pair of binoculars. He was able to see the light more clearly than with the naked eye. The colours and movement were quite definitely seen with the binoculars. He asked Cst. St-Jean and Cst. Kaminski to come and look at the object with him, but they did not think he was serious and were not interested. They said they had looked at a star, but it wasn't the object Cst. Ford was talking about. Uninterested, Cst. St-Jean and Cst. Kaminski remained at the Detachment and did not go with Cst. Ford.

Cst. Ford went to the riverbank and continued to observe the object with the binoculars. The light moved slowly and would sometimes stop completely. Cst. Ford spotted a similar light which appeared to be further away, but he didn't recall if it was moving because he only glanced at it for a minute or so. The original object he was interested in dropped below the level of the tree tops but came back up again for a short period. It then proceeded to move below the level to the tree tops again and failed to reappear. Cst. Ford had watched the strange light for about 35 to 45 minutes before it disappeared. The light moved up and down and at times would completely stop and at no time did he hear any sounds in connection with the light. Both lights disappeared at the same time.

The Detachment supervisors were not impressed with Cst. St-Jean and Cst. Kaminski's lack of interest. A subsequent police report written by Sgt. R. J. Hunter noted that it was rather disturbing that there was a lack of interest and indifference on the part of Cst. Kaminski and more particularly Cst. St-Jean who is considerably senior. Sgt. Hunter noted that both Constables were made aware of his views.

Sgt. Hunter checked on the morning of January 20 with local aircraft operations and the Department of Transportation to see if they had detected any aircraft. They advised there was no record or other information about any aircraft in operation in Inuvik around the time of Cst. Ford's observations. The Officer in Charge of the Department of Transportation office advised that if there had been unidentified aircraft in the area, at any appreciable altitude, it would have raised an alert and would have notified their office, however, this was not the case.

Sgt. Hunter noted that atmospheric conditions at the time of Cst. Ford's observations were mostly clear with stars in view. There was approximately 50% of the face of the moon showing and the temperature was -29 degrees Celsius with a trace of ice fog near the ground level. Sgt. Hunter noted that there was no further information which might account for what Cst. Ford had observed.

Inspector K. D. Smith was also not impressed at the lack of interest by Cst. St-Jean and Cst. Kaminski noting that they showed little confidence in Cst. Ford when they limited their observations to looking out a window in the general direction of the light that Cst. Ford had indicated. He suspected that it was possible Cst. St-Jean and Cst. Kaminski believed Cst. Ford was trying to play a trick on them. Insp. Smith spoke to Cst. St-Jean and Cst. Kaminski and advised them that he expects them to be more receptive to observations of their fellow members and he was satisfied that their apparent indifference in this instance was an isolated case because of the subject under discussion. Insp. Smith also makes note that he has no doubt that Cst. Ford accurately described what he had witnessed in his police report.

LUMSDEN, SASKATCHEWAN UFO SIGHTING

On October 24, 1967 in the small town of Lumsden, Saskatchewan four young persons, an adult and an RCMP officer witnessed a UFO sighting. At approximately 9:30 pm, the group of civilians reported an unidentified flying object hovering over the valley, approximately two miles southeast of Lumsden. The youth saw a small white light revolving in a looping motion and at one point the object appeared to hover over top of the valley. It disappeared for a few seconds and then reappeared in a different location over the valley.

The group left the valley and proceeded to exit "C" on highway 11. They stopped and observed a large red object in the sky approximately two feet in length which was rapidly approaching them. This object had a darker substance surrounding it. Suddenly, it faded away. The four youth were very excited and the female adult was crying and hysterical. RCMP Cst. L. C. Ferguson was dispatched to the call.

When Cst. Ferguson arrived on scene, he saw a bright red light surrounded by a series of smaller white lights. The white lights were flashing on and off in unison, in one second intervals. The object was rising at approximately a 45 degree angle skyward and slowly disappeared into the cloud cover. The whole sighting lasted for approximately three minutes. Cst. Ferguson noted that there was no sound emanating from the object.

SLAVE LAKE, ALBERTA UFO SIGHTING

On February 3, 1968 Slave Lake RCMP Cst. A. M. McLeod and Cst.

M. C. Nadeau were on patrol at 4:10 am traveling on old Highway #2 near Wagner, Alberta when they saw an unidentified flying object.

The object was round in shape and was giving off intermittent pink and white and reddish light. The object appeared to be three times larger than a star. Both RCMP officers were unable to tell how far away the object was from them, but noted that the sky was clear and that they had good visibility. The object was in the northeast part of the sky and the sighting lasted approximately 10 minutes. During that 10 minute period, Cst. McLeod and Cst. Nadeau observed the object travel half way across the sky three times at a high rate of speed. On occasion, it would suddenly stop for about one minute and remain stationary before changing its direction of travel. After approximately 10 minutes, the object gained altitude and disappeared in the northeast sky. Neither Cst. McLeod or Cst. Nadeau heard any sound emanating from the object.

PRINCE RUPERT, BRITISH COLUMBIA UFO SIGHTING

On July 28, 1968 at 11:20 pm, Prince Rupert RCMP Cst. D. W. Brown, Cst. D. D. Ferrell and Cst. K. E. Allen along with Auxiliary Cst. M. McLeod and Cst. A. Steel all witnessed a round shaped object that was orange in colour. It was moving slowly in a westerly direction at an altitude of about 4,300 feet. The sighting lasted about two and half minutes and was observed at the Parkside Motel. The officers noted that the sky was cloudy at the time of the sighting. There was no sound heard emanating from the object and it disappeared quickly once the sighting ended.

On August 6, 1968 at 12:15 am, Prince Rupert RCMP Cst. D. M. Dalziel and Cst. H. Gerrits witnessed what was described as two star-like objects but larger, both orange in colour flying at an altitude of about 3,000 feet. One object disappeared quickly upward while the other moved southward slowly until it went out of sight. The sighting lasted approximately 15 minutes.

INVERNESS, NOVA SCOTIA UFO SIGHTING

On July 20, 1968 at approximately 11:30 pm a call to the Inverness RCMP Detachment was made by a local farmer who resided on Deepdale Road. The farmer and members of his family had been watching a bright light in the sky over his farm for the past twenty minutes. The farmer called the local RCMP and advised that the object was still present in the sky and that he was requesting the RCMP look into the matter.

Cst. C. M. Campbell responded to the call for service. He saw a bright object in the sky appearing to be several miles away and at a high altitude. The object was giving off the colours of red, green and white. The object remained stationary for approximately 10 minutes according to Cst. Campbell.

The farmer and his family told Cst. Campbell that they had been out driving and when they returned home, they noticed a luminous object directly over their farm at an estimated altitude of 10,000 feet. As they pulled into their driveway, the object left in a northerly direction at a high rate of speed. It then stopped and remained stationary for approximately one hour. The object had caused the roof of the nearby barn to be lit up by the lights when they first spotted the object.

A second object was noted at the same altitude, but it was to the east of the farm. The lights from the second object lit up a corner of the field. This object also left upon the family's arrival, but it did not reappear again. The second object was similar in appearance to the first and neither objects made any sound. The exact shape of the object could not be determined due to the intensity of the light but they believed it was round.

The first object disappeared around 12:30 at a terrific rate of speed. The entire UFO sighting lasted approximately one hour and fifteen minutes. Cst. Campbell also made note that the civilian witnesses seemed reliable and that none of them had been drinking alcohol.

ROSSLAND, BRITISH COLUMBIA UFO SIGHTING

On April 27, 1968 at approximately 12:10 am, Cst. R. J. Aird and Cst. Larochelle exited the Rossland RCMP Detachment when they noticed what they thought was a moving star. The sky was clear and the light was in the direction of Red Mountain. There were two other objects sitting apart at about a 30 degree angle. The object that was moving came from between the other two lights and continued to move in an easterly direction until it vanished from sight. The constables noted that it moved at a tremendous rate of speed. The objects showed colours of red, yellow and blue-green. They couldn't determine their shape but all three objects appeared to move.

Cst. Aird went into the office and grabbed a pair of binoculars. After watching for approximately one hour, Cst. Aird and Cst. Larochelle moved toward the objects about 18 miles near Sheep Lake Junction. The objects continued to flash in the same colours and did not change in size. The constables were still unable to determine what shape these objects were. As they were observing the UFOs at the newer observation point, one of the objects moved away from them and then returned followed by lateral movements to the side and then back to its original position. Cst. Aird and Cst. Larochelle notified Castlegar RCMP Detachment personnel about the sighting, but they were already observing the objects. The objects disappeared from sight at approximately 1:00 am.

THE POSSESSION OF MAURICE THERIAULT

On February 18, 1985, the famous demonologists Ed and Lorraine Warren set out from their home in Munroe, Connecticut to speak with a tomato farmer named Maurice "Frenchy" Theriault and his family. If the names sound familiar to you, it is because they are the real life people that Hollywood portrayed in the blockbuster movies *The Conjuring* and *The Nun*.

Ed and Lorraine Warren had received a call from Father Galen Beardsley of the Saint Paul's church in Warren, Massachusetts the evening before. Father Beardsley informed them that he had been approached by Maurice Theriault and his wife Nancy at mass about strange phenomena happening to them at their farmhouse on Brimfield Road. The Warrens eagerly accepted the request for help. They brought along some back up with them for the initial meet and greet. Detective Karen Jaffe was a thirteen year police veteran working for a police department in Connecticut. She was an occult criminal subject matter expert who had met and befriended the Warrens. She had wanted to help them investigate a case and the Warrens felt they could use her assistance in the Theriault case.

The Warrens and Detective Jaffe sat in the Theriault's kitchen listening to Nancy tell them about the abusive life that Maurice had endured throughout the years and the types of supernatural occurrences she and he had experienced. Some of these occurrences included Maurice being seen by witnesses at different locations during the exact same time period, crucifixes bleeding from the palms and feet of Jesus Christ, Maurice having prophetic feelings and dreams and many strange behaviours by Maurice including speaking Latin in which he was not fluent in.

When Nancy spoke about Maurice's mother being murdered by his father, Maurice began to cry. Detective Jaffe was the first person to observe that Maurice was crying tears of blood. The bleeding stopped when Maurice stopped crying. He wept tears of blood several times during the initial interview.

On February 24, 1985 Police Chief Jerry Seibert was working at the Warren Police Department when Maurice Theriault surrendered two Winchester rifles and a shotgun. Theriault told Police Chief Seibert that he had seen a psychic who told him he was possessed. Theriault fearing he may inappropriately use the firearms felt it best to turn them over to local law enforcement.

Maurice had become the talk of the town. There had been a series of small fires at Maurice's farm house in which both the Warren Police Department and State Fire Marshal's Office believed were deliberately set. Maurice was telling the towns folk that his house was possessed and that a mysterious force was responsible for the fires and objects moving around his house.

Chief Seibert received a disturbance call at the Theriault residence being reported by Maurice's wife Nancy. Chief Seibert and his friend, Massachusetts State Trooper Colin Kerns, responded to the call for service. Upon arrival, they were greeted by Nancy who appeared terrified. Maurice was sitting at his kitchen table with blood on his chin. Chief Seibert and Trooper Kerns saw blood smeared on the bathroom floor and in the tub of the Theriault's washroom. Both Chief Seibert and Trooper Kerns witnessed blood start to stream from Maurice's eyes. Chief Seibert also noticed the sign of the cross protruding from Maurice's blood stained t-shirt.

Nancy provided a statement to Chief Seibert where she said she heard bizarre sounds coming from the washroom and when she opened the door to check on Maurice, she located him lying in the middle of a pool of blood. He was lying on his back with his face contorted, eyes rolled back into his head and his teeth exposed. Blood was bubbling from the corner of his mouth as he spoke what she described to be an unknown foreign language. She disclosed to the police officers that she and her daughter had seen an apparition of Maurice on another occasion. Nancy also described an incident where Maurice displayed super human strength and lifted a two ton farm tractor on his own accord.

Chief Seibert telephoned Father Beardsley. Father Beardsley was already familiar with Maurice because he had been working with Ed and Lorraine Warren on his case. Father Beardsley advised Chief Seibert that he would contact the Warren's and update them on the situation.

On May 2, 1985 the exorcism of Maurice Theriault was set to take place at the Brimfield Road farmhouse. Among the team of investigators accompanying Ed and Lorraine Warren was Hartford Police detective Kent Burch who volunteered his time with the Warrens. Bishop Robert McKenna would be the Roman Catholic authority tasked with performing the exorcism.

The exorcism was filmed by police detective Burch and can be viewed in part on the Internet, he witnessed several supernatural events. Maurice Theriault's eyes bled and his skin cracked and split open, the sound of the headboard in the master bedroom smashed violently against the wall, indiscernible human voices were heard chattering in the kitchen, phantom car doors were heard slamming shut, crosses appeared as if they had been burnt into Maurice's hands and when his boots were removed, the signs of stigmata bleeding were seen through his white socks. The exorcism had been deemed a success and clairvoyant Lorraine Warren felt the demonic presence had dissipated.

Two months after Maurice Theriault's exorcism, Chief Seibert had received information that Maurice Theriault had sexually assaulted his stepdaughter. His stepdaughter had made a disclosure to a child abuse investigator; however, she said it was the doppelganger of Maurice. Chief Seibert believed that it was a minimization tactic by the stepdaughter rather than a case of demonic possession. Maurice, nonetheless, turned himself into Chief Seibert at the Warren Police Department. While Maurice was sitting in the room with Chief Seibert, he witnessed blood start to seep out of Maurice's mouth and bubble out of his nose. Chief Seibert prepared Maurice to be transferred to the court house in Spencer, Massachusetts.

While Chief Seibert was processing Maurice at the court house, a court officer approached Chief Seibert in a panic and told him to come quickly. Again, Maurice was bleeding from his mouth and eyes and taking convulsions which prompted the court house staff to call an ambulance. Maurice was rushed to the hospital in Worcester.

Maurice Theriault was not convicted of any crimes against his step daughter. She was reluctant to testify against Maurice and the District Attorney's office was hesitant to prosecute after seeing the exorcism video.

Just as his father had done several years ago, Maurice Theriault killed himself with a self-inflicted gunshot wound to the head on November 3, 1992. Before his demise, he had shot and wounded his wife Nancy. Nancy managed to stagger to a neighbour's residence before collapsing and being transported to the hospital. Whether supernatural or not, Maurice Theriault was indeed haunted by demons.

THE HAUNTED POLICE STATION

In the town of Jamshedpur located in the state of Jharkhand, India is a police station said to be haunted by wandering spirits. The Jamshedpur Police station is situated on Tata - Hata Main Road. Sub Inspector S. Baske released a statement to the media saying that the police officers posted at this particular police station have been routinely organizing prayers and making offerings to invisible spirits in order to ward off the ghosts who haunt the police station. The police station was allegedly built on land that was used as a Hindu cremation ground by local villagers.

All of the personnel who work at the station depart the building each day by 11:00 pm. Officers are terrified to stay in the building once darkness falls. They have reported hearing strange noises from inside the police station once night falls with an increase in supernatural activity occurring just before midnight. Sub Inspector Baske also stated that during the evening, the telephone lines often stop working despite being checked and repaired on multiple occasions.

BLACKETTS LAKE, NOVA SCOTIA

Blacketts Lake is a small community located in Cape Breton Regional Municipality. The community is said to have been named after Walter Blackett, who was one of the two sons of William Blackett. The Blackett's originated from London, England and immigrated to Prince Edward Island, Canada in the 1780's. Walter Blackett and his wife moved from PEI and established themselves and their nine children on the shores of Blacketts Lake.

One night in the late summer of 1994 or 1995, retired Corporal Patrick Murphy of the RCMP and his wife Candace had a supernatural experience in Blacketts Lake. Cpl. Murphy is not a believer in the supernatural. He was a police officer with the Royal Canadian Mounted Police for over twenty years and has driven some remote roads, but still to this day he cannot explain what he and Candace saw.

Cpl. Murphy and his wife were just teenagers and not married at the time. After a late evening of movie watching, Cpl. Murphy drove Candace home in his parent's car. It was approximately 3:00 am, when Cpl. Murphy and Candace reached the T intersection near the church. Cpl. Murphy and Candace saw two identical twin girls with long blond hair. They were both wearing olden day white dresses and carrying baskets. They looked like they were having fun as they were running through Bobby Barrington's property. Cpl. Murphy asked Candace what the hell two little girls were doing outside so late at night. Suddenly, the two twin girls saw Cpl. Murphy's vehicle approaching and they both stopped moving.

Candace said that it was almost as if the two girls had never seen a vehicle before. They simply stood there and peered straight into Cpl. Murphy and Candace's vehicle. Candace was scared and told Cpl. Murphy to keep driving. Candace looked back at where the two girls were standing, but they were both gone. Cpl. Murphy dropped Candace off at her house.

Cpl. Murphy said if he had been a police officer at that time, he probably would have stopped and interacted with the two girls, but at the time he was 18 or 19 years old and he was a little freaked out. Cpl. Murphy did drive back the same way but he didn't see anyone during his return trip. Both Cpl. Murphy and Candace were completely sober at the time of the sighting. Cpl. Murphy and Candace described the apparitions as being completely solid. According to Cpl. Murphy's mother, Bobby Barrington never had any children. Local folklore states that seven of the Blackett's kids went out onto the lake in a raft and drowned. Two of the Blackett kids were said to have been twins.

Another strange story surrounding Blacketts Lake is about a female from Ontario, Canada who decided to fly to Sydney, Nova Scotia on a whim. She didn't have any family or friends in Cape Breton nor had she ever previously stepped foot on the island. Upon landing in Sydney, she took a taxi out to Blacketts Lake and committed suicide by drowning herself in Blacketts Lake.

Blacketts Lake is a paranormal hotbed of activity. Adventurers have reported that their compasses will not function properly around Coxheath Mountain which is connected to Blacketts Lake. Strange lights have been reported over the lake and surrounding area. Many individuals have also reported being followed by a dark entity or hearing terrible screams coming from the area late at night, such as witness John Reppa.

John reported that in the early spring of 1977, he and his friend Lawrence were in Blacketts Lake on their way to a dance in East Bay. They had taken a pint of rum from Lawrence's sister's house but decided to stash it near an alder tree by the little bridge that connects to the Sydney River. They were afraid of getting caught with the rum at one of the police road checks on the way to the dance.

Around 1:00 am or 2:00 am, Lawrence and John decide to return to the alder tree to pick up the pint of rum. They got into Lawrence's yellow Vega car and returned to Blacketts Lake. They stopped at the spot where they stashed the rum bottle and exited the vehicle. They went to retrieve the bottle of rum, but it was gone. They began searching the immediate area, but to no avail. Thinking that the bottle slid out underneath the snow somewhere, they retrieved a shovel from Lawrence's car. As they approached the last known location of the bottle of rum, they heard a loud high-pitched scream or howl.

Lawrence and John both froze in fear. The squealing scream lasted approximately 15 seconds as the pitch becoming lower and lower. John described the voice as being really abrasive and horrible. The scream stopped after echoing off of the hills. Fearing for their safety, Lawrence and John jumped back into the vehicle and left.

The following day, John returned to the scene with his uncle. He had his uncle pull over to where he and Lawrence had stashed the bottle of rum. To his amazement, the pint of rum was in the exact same spot where he and Lawrence had left it.

The experience left an impact on John. So much so, years later he began researching the area at the Beaton Institute. He was able to learn that the original Blackett family were the first white settlers in the area and that they had experienced strange phenomena. The Blackett family had experienced items moving, disappearing and reappearing and they also heard the terrible howl.

The great granddaughter of Walter Blackett, Isabel Blackett Kennedy reports that while her great grandfather was building a cabin on Blacketts Lake, strange phenomena began occurring. One morning carpenters and masons found stones from the wall knocked out and strewn about the ground, but no foot-prints were seen. Neighbors took turns watching Blackett's property, but the nights were silent. They neighbors decided to sprinkle sand around the house and return home. The following morning, stones were once again knocked out and thrown around. There were no foot-prints in the sand either.

On another evening, Elizabeth, Margaret and Isabel, three granddaughters of Walter Blackett decided to go to the construction site of the cabin in hopes of seeing the ghost. They looked into the dim cellar and saw a dark figure moving from one of the corners. It unleashed an ungodly sound. The three girls ran away and told their family. The family rounded up some neighbors armed with a rifle, lanterns and pitchforks. Upon returning the property however, a great stone from the cellar had been thrown over a wall and lay on the ground. Nothing else was disturbed. The cabin was never completed and Walter Beckett passed away.

Local paranormal investigator Jason Murphy told me that one of his friends had seen an apparition described as the woman in white who appears on the bridge near the Sydney River. The sighting scared Jason's friend so bad that he still to this day will not drive around Blacketts Lake.

ST. CLEMENS ANGLICAN CHURCH

In 1992, the late Gerry Oram purchased an old church which had been converted into a home. Oram was retired from the Royal Canadian Mounted Police. He described himself as a logical person. The home was approximately 100 years old and used to be the St. Clemens Anglican Church in Saint John, New Brunswick.

Oram spoke of several supernatural events which occurred within the home. The house contained several typical haunting characteristics according to Oram, such as the feeling of cold spots and the smell of tobacco and lemons. He described seeing several apparitions during his time in the home as well. He once saw an older woman with curly hair wearing a dark colored hat, a grey dress with a black smock placed over it and black socks. As an artist, Oram sketched the apparition which had been identified as an old Anglican nun by one of his local friends.

On another occasion, Oram witnessed an even more compelling event. He had fallen asleep on his living room couch when he was awoken at 3:00 am to an apparition of a little girl. He saw a little girl with her arms crossed and her legs folded levitating in mid-air. She wore a white hat, white stockings and black leather shoes. Even more incredible, Oram spoke to the little girl. He asked the apparition if there was anything he could do for her. The little girl said that she was eight years old and that her name was Marie Wilson. She told Oram that he could visit her grave. She disappeared before telling him anything further. The following day, Oram began researching Marie Wilson. He was only able to locate a 25 year old

Marie Wilson's grave in one of the Catholic cemeteries. Eight year old Marie Wilson remained a haunting mystery to Oram.

Oram wasn't the only person in the house who experienced anything supernatural. On one occasion, he had two friends staying with him from New York. One of his friends was woken up at 3:00 am and witnessed the apparition of a young man who was bent over staring at him. Oram's friend described the apparition as a young male wearing a tweed hat and pantaloons. Even more unnerving was the fact that Oram's friend had placed his sleeping bag in the exact same spot where the congregation use to place the coffins during funeral services.

Oram swore he witnessed hundreds of supernatural events at his home. The property certainly has the history to be a haunted location. Churches are well known places for celebrating both life and death. A lot of human emotion and energy passes through a location like that. Oram passed away in 2006. Perhaps he has finally received the resolve that he sought regarding little eight year old Marie Wilson.

On April 6, 2019 my mother, Kim Farrell, contacted me regarding official Paranormal Phenomena Research & Investigation business. She stated that she had just received a call from her step daughter Annie Farrell asking if anything strange or unusual has ever happened at her residence on Quarry Island. Mom told her no and asked her why. Annie said she and her boyfriend Colton Shaw were watching mom's house on Quarry Island for her during the week of March 25, 2019. On one particular evening, at 3:20 am, Colton heard footsteps coming downstairs toward the bed in the basement. He also heard the sound of a windbreaker rubbing against similar material. Something ice cold touched his left thigh, hip, rib and shoulder. No apparition was seen and Colton wasn't sure if he was complete awake or not at the time of the incident.

On April 15, 2019 I interviewed Annie and Colton separately at the PPRI office. Annie stated that at the end of March at around 3:20 am, she and Colton were downstairs in the basement sleeping. She was having a nightmare and heard a loud bang but couldn't wake up. The loud bang turned out to be Colton dropping his cellphone. She felt Colton put his arm around her. The nightmare ended and she rolled over and saw that Colton was wide awake. She could tell that something was wrong with him. She asked him if he was ok. He didn't want to tell her what was wrong because it would scare her. After pressing him for information, he said that something touched him four times from his hip to his shoulder and it was cold. He also said he heard the sound of a windbreaker. She said that there was no one else in the house at the time and mom's cat Lucy was upstairs. She was familiar with the house and had never experienced anything like this before.

During Colton's interview, he too couldn't remember the exact date of when this incident occurred but stated that it was sometime during the end of March 2019 around 3:00 am. While he was sleeping, he could hear the sound of rubbing from a windbreaker coming down the basement stairs. Colton wasn't sure if he was completely awake during the incident. He stated that when he initially heard the sound coming down the stairs, he recalled being on the inside of the bed. The sound stopped and then turned around. He assumed it was Annie's father Ken coming home. A few moments later however, he heard the same windbreaker sound come all the way around to the bed. Colton was now on the outside of the bed facing toward Annie and the wall. Whatever or whoever was making the sound was approaching Colton's back. The sound suddenly stopped. Whatever or whoever was approaching the bed was now standing directly behind Colton in the dark basement. He was too afraid to look behind him, so he continued to lie in bed, quiet with his eyes tightly closed. Suddenly he felt an ice cold touch on his thigh, hip, rib and then shoulder. Colton then heard the sound of the windbreaker begin to walk away. Once the sound disappeared, he looked around the basement but could only see the dimly lit fire in the woodstove. Annie woke up and asked him if he was ok.

On April 21, 2019 I travelled to Quarry Island and checked the area where Colton and Annie had their experience. Utilizing the Electromagnetic Field Radiation Detector and Forward Infrared thermal camera thermometer, I did not pick up any anomalous readings.

Although Colton did not see an apparition, he did experience some common haunting characteristics. He heard or perceived the sound of footsteps and a windbreaker or tracksuit jacket material rubbing against the same type of material as if someone was walking. He also experienced the ice-cold sensation of something touching his thigh, hip, rib and shoulder. The only issue with this report was that initially when he heard the footsteps on the stairs and the sound of the tracksuit, he stated that he was lying on the inside of the bed. However, he was actually on the outside of the bed which leads him to believe he was dreaming during the first experience. He also wasn't sure if he was totally awake during the second experience which leads to an alternate explanation for his experience, hypnopompic dreaming.

Hypnopompic hallucinations occur when an individual is waking. The hallucination can include smell, taste, tactile, vision or sound sensations which are experienced only in the individual's mind, and not by others. In this case file, Annie did not hear the footsteps or the windbreaker sound nor did she feel the cold sensation. Colton admits in his statement that he must have been asleep during the first incident because Annie was on the inside of the bed toward the wall while he was on the outside. He also said that when he heard the second sounds, he was in between being awake and asleep. Hypnopompic hallucinations can feel very real and the individual may even believe that they have really seen or felt something.

Another theory is backed up by some previous paranormal

experiences involving my mother and another one of her residences. Often times when we think of a haunting, we think of places, in particular; inns, castles, historic properties, battlefields and homes. Those are all common places where ghosts dwell. We often neglect to think about persons being haunted or having spirits attracted or attached to them.

My dad, Neil Van Dusen, had a bleeding disorder called Hemophilia B and he learned in 1994 that he had contracted hepatitis C through tainted blood and blood products as a youth growing up in Ottawa, Ontario. The hepatitis C caused severe fatigue and my father would often need to go for a nap during the day. It wouldn't be uncommon for anyone present or visiting the house to see Neil emerge from the master bedroom and walk down the hallway toward the kitchen to make a cup of coffee after one of his naps. He passed away on August 14th, 2006 due to complications from hepatitis C. Family friend Lucene MacIntyre was visiting my mother in Lower Sackville at 133 Lumsden Crescent, Lower Sackville, Nova Scotia after my father had passed away. Lucene heard footsteps coming from the upstairs hallway and when she turned her head, she saw Neil standing near the master bedroom. She described his appearance as being the same as before he had passed away. Although he was only forty-eight years old, the hepatitis C had ravaged his body and aged him beyond his years.

On another occasion, my mother's new husband Ken Farrell had a paranormal encounter with dad in the same Lower Sackville home. While Ken was sitting in the upstairs living room on the couch, he turned his head to look toward the hallway and saw Neil.

Ken described him as looking unmistakably younger than he did when he passed away.

The third experience involved friends of my mothers, Judy Rigel and her son Barron. My mother had to run out for a few minutes and left Judy and Barron alone. They went downstairs and found a guitar. They began playing around with the guitar when all of a sudden, they felt an ice-cold gust of wind come from the upstairs of the residence, down to the split entry way and continue further downward toward the basement. The ice-cold feeling went through Judy and Barron. Barron told his mother that he felt the ice-cold sensation as well. Judy who is sensitive and a Reiki master, spoke out loud and said something similar to; "Neil, it is okay. Kim gave us permission to be here." The ice-cold feeling dissipated and nothing else occurred.

From a parapsychological investigative standpoint, due to the limited evidence that was available during Colton and Annie's experience, it remains undetermined whether or not it was an apparitional experience or a hypnopompic experience.

THE HAUNTING OF COLBORNE LODGE

Colborne Lodge is located in the City of Toronto's High Park. It was built in 1836 and deeded to the City of Toronto in 1890 after socialite John George Howard passed away. Today it is a historical museum open to the public situated at 11 Colborne Lodge Drive.

In 1969, a Toronto Police Service officer assigned to the motorcycle section was patrolling High Park. He parked near Colborne Lodge to complete some paperwork. The officer noticed some movement out of the corner of his eye. Looking toward one of the upstairs Lodge windows, he saw a small female wearing what he described to be period attire. Just as quick as he had seen the lady in the window, she had disappeared. Knowing that the lodge was closed to the public at this hour, he commenced a foot patrol around the property. All of the doors and windows were deemed to be secure. The police officer was confident that there was nobody present in the Lodge and began to second guess what he had seen.

The following day, he kept thinking about what he had seen. He decided to return to the lodge which was now open to the public. While touring the lodge, he disclosed to a female employee that he had seen a small female wearing period attire looking out of one of the second story windows. The employee showed the police officer a picture of John Howard's wife, Jemima. The police officer confirmed to the lodge employee that the lady he had seen in the window was Jemima. She had died in 1877 after a battle with breast cancer in the same bedroom that the police officer had seen the apparition. A tomb situated across from Colborne Lodge contains

John and Jemima Howard's remains. Museum co-ordinator Cheryl Hart said that many visitors have reported seeing something move out of the corner of their eye, sensing a presence or report being touched while touring the lodge.

INDIO HILLS, CALIFORNIA UFO SIGHTING

By the 1970's the UFO phenomena had gained world-wide attention, literally. The United Nations General Assembly decision 33/426 proposed creating an investigative agency to coordinate on a national level, the scientific research and investigation into extraterrestrial life, including unidentified flying objects, and to inform the Secretary-General of the observations, research and evaluation of such activities.

On the evening of April 5, 1977 between 9 pm and 10 pm, multiple reports of flying saucers were reported to have been seen by Coachella Valley residents and law enforcement personnel. It was the second sighting of UFOs in less than a month. In the early morning hours on March 23, 1977 a yellow-reddish object was seen streaking through the skies by a dozen law enforcement officers situated in the Valley, Riverside and Los Angeles areas. One Deputy described the UFO as a cigar with lights on either end.

The April 5th sighting had more details observed by the witness. Several civilians reported seeing three or four circular shaped objects "like a saucer upside down" measuring approximately 100 feet long and two stories high. They had blinking red lights and hovered approximately 100 feet above the ground for at least a half hour. The objects sped away at speeds upwards of 110 miles an hour.

The Federal Aviation Administration control tower situated at the Palm Springs Airport had no reported sightings. The Indio police had 15 people call to report the UFO sighting around 9:00 pm.

A California Highway Patrol Officer named Tom Granger was driving along Interstate 10 Highway toward Indio at 9:30 pm when he saw what he initially thought were four jets. Officer Granger said the objects had red flashing lights on the bottom of them and made a sweeping manoeuvre to the left and then to the right. He recognized the objects were not emitting any noise which he thought was strange. Based on the movement of the objects and the lack of sound being emitted, Officer Granger deducted that these were not conventional aircraft.

It is not uncommon for certain locations to be inundated with UFO sightings for a short period of time. Whether the geographical area is being bombarded with meteor showers or extraterrestrial visitors, these strange sightings can be witnessed over several consecutive nights.

Other locations are dubbed “UFO hot spots” where it is common to witness UFO sightings on a frequent basis. The small town of Rachel, Nevada is a well-known UFO hot spot. It is located approximately 45 kilometres from the not so secret United States Air Force facility known as Area 51, Dreamland, Paradise Ranch, the Ranch, Watertown, Groom Lake, and the Nevada Test and Training Range. Its official name is Homey Airport and has been assigned airport identifier code KXTA. It is no wonder this area is a UFO hot spot. The U.S. Air Force is known to test experimental aircrafts at this facility.

THE MURDER OF TERESITA BASA

Occasionally when conventional police investigative techniques are exhausted, detectives and investigators will resort to unconventional techniques such as the use of psychic detectives.

One of the most interesting police investigations involving the use of a psychic is the Teresita Basa homicide. The case has been written about by many authors, newspapers and was even features on the popular television series *Unsolved Mysteries*.

On February 21, 1977 Chicago Police Department detectives Joe Stachula and Lee Epplen caught the homicide case of Teresita Basa. Basa was found in her high-rise apartment stabbed multiple times with a kitchen knife, wrapped in bed linen and set on fire. A mattress had been put overtop of her and the crime scene was made to look like a robbery and sexual assault. An autopsy would later provide evidence that Basa had not been sexually assaulted. In fact, there was very little forensic evidence left behind at the crime scene. The detectives located a note with the initials A. S. on it indicating that the person who had written the note was supposed to provide Basa with some theatre tickets. The homicide investigation went cold until Detectives Stachula and Epplen received a call from the Evanston Police Department approximately 19 miles north of Chicago.

Evanston Police advised that they had spoken with Dr. Jose Chua and his wife Remibias and that they should speak to the immediately about the Basa homicide investigation.

Basa worked as a raspatory therapist at the currently defunct Edgewater Hospital. Coincidentally, Dr. Chua and his wife Remibias also worked at Edgewater Hospital. Remibias Chua worked in the same department as Basa, but the two women did not know one another.

One evening in July 1977, Dr. Chua found his wife laying on their bed talking in a strange voice that was not her own. Remibias Chua claimed that she was a woman named Teresita Basa and that she had been murdered by a co-worker named Allan Showery. Remibias Chua said Showery had stolen some jewellery from her apartment. When Remibias Chua came out of her trance like state, she didn't remember anything she had said. Dr. Chua and his wife were embarrassed by this incident and decided not to report it to the police at the time.

A couple of days later, Remibias Chua had a second episode. The spirit of Teresita Basa asked the Chua's to bring her killer to justice and provided specific information that Showery had stolen a pearl ring from Basa during the homicide and had given it to his girlfriend. Names and phone numbers of individuals who could identify the jewellery as belonging to Basa were also provided by the spirit of Basa.

In August 1977, Remibias Chua had a third incident in which Teresita Basa allegedly possessed her body. It was after this episode that Dr. Chua and his wife decided to contact the local police.

Detectives Stachula and Epplen were curious about the name Allan Showery as they had found a note in Basa's apartment with the initials A. S. on it. After conducting some enquires, they learned that Allan Showery was an orderly at Edgewater Hospital where the Chua's and Basa worked.

Detectives Stachula and Epplen attended Showery's apartment situated at 630 West Schubert and invited Showery to attend the police station for questioning. He provided an alibi stating that he was scheduled to attend Basa's apartment the evening she was murdered to fix a television set for her, but she had cancelled on him. It wasn't until Detectives Stachula and Epplen spoke to Showery's girlfriend, Yanka Kamluk that his alibi began to unravel. Kamluk disclosed to Detectives Stachula and Epplen that Showery had given her a pearl ring and a jade necklace as a late Christmas gift and that he knew nothing about fixing electronic devices.

Detectives called the list of individuals whom the spirit of Basa had stated could identify her stolen jewelry. They attended the police station and positively identified the jewelry seized from Yanka Kamluk as belonging to Basa.

Detectives Stachula and Epplen used this information to elicit a confession from Showery. Showery confessed and was tried in January 1979. It ended in a mistrial because the jury was deadlocked on their decision. Showery plead guilty before the start of the second trial and received 22 years total for his crimes.

Skeptics have criticized Remibias Chua's extraordinary claims saying that she made up the spiritual connection with Basa. Remibias Chua worked with both Basa and Showery at Edgewater Hospital and information had been discovered that she attended a party once before at Basa's apartment. Furthermore, Showery had allegedly made complaints about the quality of Remibias Chua's work at the hospital and she was feeling threatened and frightened by Showery. Even Detective Stachula expressed skepticism about the mediumship of Remibias Chua but was quoted as saying "Nonetheless, everything here is completely true."

THE PSYCHIC COP

It is not an unusual concept that police departments resort to the use of psychic mediums when all other conventional investigative techniques have been exhausted. There are several parapsychological studies to suggest that certain individuals possess above average psi abilities. Mediums are sensitive to their environment and can detect and collect information in which non-sensitive individuals or technological equipment cannot.

I equate the use of a medium in a paranormal investigation to the police using a confidential informant in a criminal investigation. You receive the information, document the information and then take the necessary steps to try and corroborate as much of it as possible. How valuable or relative the information will be to the field investigation depends on what you can corroborate. Sometimes information such as names or deaths can even be verified through historical records or vital statistics.

This type of investigative technique holds more weight if the medium being utilized goes into the investigation blind. Otherwise, any evidence collected is purely based on a trust factor that the medium hasn't conducted any prior research. Information which appears to be inaccurate or which cannot be corroborated should still be documented and disclosed. You never know when the information may become relevant.

An example of this can be seen in a New York City homicide investigation from 1976. Psychic Dorothy Allison who is now deceased, reported seeing the word "Mar", the number "222" and oil connected to a missing girl. At the time, the information couldn't be corroborated by the police. Two years later, the NYPD located the missing girl's body at a remote location on Staten Island. Her body was found in an oil drum with the number 222 stamped on it next to a rock with the word "Mar" written on it.

The Metropolitan Police in London, England took unconventional techniques one step further when one of their own officer's claimed to be a "Psychic Cop". Retired Detective Constable Keith Wright, who now uses the name Keith Charles, was a police officer with the Metropolitan Police for 32 years. He earned the nickname "Psychic Cop" after claiming he had clairvoyant abilities in which he used to solve criminal cases while working as a detective.

One of the more impressive cases he worked on was assisting the London Transport Police with a homicide investigation. Detective Inspector Alan Wilson consulted Charles over the suspicious death of a man which had taken place during a party at the Ministry of Defence building in Kensington. Charles instructed Detective Inspector Wilson to send him a photograph of the victim in a sealed envelope. Even though Charles was miraculously able to provide at least 30 details relevant to the investigation, he did not provide anything that directly helped solve the case.

Charles envisioned the victim falling down stairs and landing in the basement. The victim had been located at the bottom of a basement shaft. Charles also saw a bank, a female and a taxi being involved in the crime. Detective Inspector Wilson was impressed because the banking information, female and taxi was holdback information. Holdback information is any piece of information or detail that would only be known by the perpetrator, a material witness, if any, and a select few detectives. This information is protected through non-disclosure rules so that the integrity of the investigation can be upheld. Detective Inspector Wilson said that the victim had left the party at one point to take some money out from an ATM. The victim then put the female into a taxi.

Charles also provided Detective Inspector Wilson with the correct names and descriptions of people who had attended the party, including the killer. Although the information provided by Charles was accurate and could be corroborated through investigative methods, the information was subjective hearsay and not admissible in court. Nonetheless, he went into the investigation blind and impressively provided the police with accurate information.

THE NASS VALLEY BIG FOOT

In late October 2015, Royal Canadian Mounted Police Corporal Nathan Dame stationed at the Lisims Nass Valley detachment was on patrol. While traveling from New Aiyansh to Greenville on a long, remote stretch of highway, something jumped out in front of his patrol car. Cpl. Dame saw what he described as being a creature standing approximately 10 feet tall, with dark chocolate brown hair, long arms that stretched past its waist and long legs. He was adamant that it wasn't a moose or a bear. The creature had leapt from shoulder to shoulder, straight across the highway before slowly disappearing into the forest. Cpl. Dame stopped on the highway and looked into the trees where he had last seen the creature; however, it had mysteriously disappeared. He was positive that what he had seen was a Sasquatch.

Cpl. Dame had a second experience on the exact same highway, 5 kilometers from his first sighting in early November. He was sitting in his patrol car while pulled over on the side of the highway when he heard a noise coming from the forest. Approximately twenty metres away from him, he saw something large and brown crouch down behind a tree. He got out of his vehicle to investigate, but didn't find anything. He said the forested area wasn't thick and he was positive it wasn't a moose or a bear standing on its hind legs. Cpl. Dame had inquired with some of the locals from Greenville who told stories that they too had seen a Sasquatch in the area. In fact, the area itself is something straight out of a horror novel. Not only is it a known hotspot for Bigfoot sightings,

Nass Valley is slightly north from the 720 kilometre corridor of Highway 16, commonly referred to as the Highway of Tears. The area is well known for at least three identified serial killers and a strange pattern of disappearances and murders dating as far back as 1970.

Approximately 106 kilometers south of Nass Valley lay Skeena Valley where some of the earliest Bigfoot prints in Canada have been obtained. In 1976, a dozen 15.5 inch long and 6.5 inch wide tracks with a seven foot stride were found by some local children near a slough. In August 2008, Larry Sommerfield located a footprint in a gravel pit east of Kitselas First Nation's Gitaus subdivision. He made a cast of the 16 inch footprint. It was 10.5 inches wide and Sommerfield estimated it belonged to a creature weighting at least 1,000 pounds.

If any province in Canada could hide a cryptozoological creature such as a Sasquatch, it would be British Columbia. The province is 235 million acres in size with 149 million acres or approximately 64% of the land being forested. New species of plants and insects are still being discovered by scientists exploring the region.

South Florida police Detective Rob McGinley and his wife Jennifer wanted to take a break from their hectic life. After being promoted from the Violent Crime Unit to the Homicide Unit, Detective McGinley couldn't disagree with his wife that he had been extremely overworked. Mrs. McDeavitt-McGinley had also been running herself ragged as a local business owner. Mrs. McDeavitt-McGinley suggested that they take a restful weekend in beautiful Savannah, Georgia. He had never been there, so he was open to the idea. Jennifer had just one more twist to the weekend. She suggested that they stay in a haunted bed and breakfast. Savannah, Georgia has a very haunted history. Neither Detective McGinley nor Jennifer were believers in the paranormal, but thought that it would be fun nonetheless. As a police officer, Detective McGinley always looked for reasonable and rational explanations.

Detective McGinley researched many bed and breakfasts in the area closest to the local tourist attractions and he and Jennifer had planned to see. One particular bed and breakfast toted a specific room within the house known for its haunting activity. He figured if they were going to stay at a haunted bed and breakfast, they might as well go big or stay home.

He called the bed and breakfast and spoke to the booking clerk. Detective McGinley stated that he wanted to stay in the haunted room with his wife. The booking clerk tried to dissuade Detective McGinley several times from staying in that particular room. Detective McGinley was also warned that if he decided to take the room, he would not be allowed to switch rooms during the weekend as they were almost at capacity and expected to be sold out. The booking clerk also warned that they only rent the room out if someone requests it and that it was non-refundable, even if they suddenly cancelled part way during the rental. Detective McGinley figured that the bed and breakfast was exaggerating the stories behind the room as part of the attraction.

As the weekend arrived, Detective McGinley and his wife found themselves checking into the bed and breakfast. The booking clerk remembered speaking to him on the telephone. The clerk advised Detective McGinley that they had received a cancellation for another room and he was wondering if he and his wife would be interested in that one instead. Detective McGinley and Jennifer laughed and said that they would stick with their original room.

The clerk passed him the room keys and warned him that he wouldn't be working over the weekend but would be back on Monday morning during checkout. The clerk said that he would be interested in hearing how their stay went and wished them the best of luck.

Detective McGinley and Jennifer made their way upstairs to their room with their luggage. They entered the room and found it to be very beautiful and welcoming. They both laughed and joked about the fact that they probably had overpaid for the legend of the room. They dropped their bags off and left to go and explore the local area.

Late that evening, they returned to the bed and breakfast. Detective McGinley went into the washroom and shut the door tightly. A few moments after he was in there, someone was jiggling the door handle as if to come into the washroom. He walked over to the door when suddenly it slammed open and hit him in his left knee. He laughed thinking his wife was playing a joke on him. She was in the bed, sitting straight up with her eyes wide open. She had heard the door handle being jiggled and had observed the door open on its own. They dismissed it and retired for the evening.

During the night, Detective McGinley woke up and saw a female apparition standing by the room's television set. She was wearing a black dress with a black veil. He closed his eyes and looked again, but she was still there. He closed his eyes again and looked a second time and this time the female was gone. He told himself that he must have been dreaming and again dismissed the event.

The following morning Detective McGinley made his way downstairs for a cup of coffee. A bed and breakfast employee asked him how his stay was going. Detective McGinley told them that everything was fine and that they had no issues. Detective McGinley and his wife left the bed and breakfast for the day.

They returned later in the afternoon. Detective McGinley put his cell phone in a tray with a 2 or 3 inch lip near the flat screen TV. He and Jennifer were sorting all of their purchases when suddenly his cell phone went flying across the room approximately 3 feet. He didn't see the phone being thrown, but Jennifer did. He laughed about it and said “I guess we are getting our money’s worth.”

Later that evening while Detective McGinley and Mrs. McDeavitt-McGinley were sleeping, he woke up to his wife shaking and asking something to “Please stop!”. He jumped up out of bed and saw that Jennifer was lying in the bed with the blanket tucked in on both sides of her. She told Detective McGinley that it felt like hands were tucking her in all night. The first couple of times, she was sleeping and somewhat ignored the feeling, but this time she was awake when it happened. She asked him to change rooms in the morning as she didn’t want to spend another night in the room.

In the morning, Detective McGinley asked the bed and breakfast staff if he and his wife could change rooms, however, they had no availability. They mentioned the no refund policy which Detective McGinley was accepting of since he had previously agreed to it. He and Jennifer continued to stay in the room. That evening, Jennifer continued to be tucked in by an unseen force. On at least two occasions, the blankets had also been ripped off of the bed.

On the last evening of their not so restful weekend getaway, Detective McGinley and his wife were returning to the bed and breakfast from dinner. As they approached the front door, Detective McGinley got the key ready. The front door was a heavy door with an auto locking mechanism attached to it which required a key to get into the lobby area to prevent any non-guests from entering. As they approached the front door, there was another couple on the front steps. As they approached the door, it opened wide and stayed in the open position.

"Wow, welcome back! She must really like you guys," said the clerk working the front counter.

Detective McGinley asked who "she" was. The clerk told him that it was the lady of the house who had passed away in the residence. The clerk said that if she likes guests, she makes them feel welcomed. Detective McGinley said that he will never stay at that bed and breakfast again. As for Mrs. McDeavitt-McGinley, she is now a believer in ghosts and has told everyone about their experiences. They have since been back to Savannah, though they choose to stay at another location.

Detective Rob McGinley had experienced another supernatural encounter while assigned to the Violent Crimes Division. He and some members of his unit attended a suicide in which a man had hung himself in front of his house from a tree.

The front door was also locked, so Detective McGinley walked to the back of the residence and peered through the glass window of the back door. This door was locked too, but he could see several envelopes with names printed on them and a note on the counter. The neighbours had told the police that the deceased had a girlfriend, but they didn't know where she was. Fearing that she may be in distress inside the residence, Detective McGinley requested some breaching tools in order to gain entry.

A couple of officers brought the breaching tools to the back door. As the police prepared for entry, Detective McGinley noticed that the deadbolt was now unlocked. The door handle was also unlocked. The officers on scene were perplexed. They opened the door and entered the residence. Officers began systematically searching each room and closet. They also searched the attic and crawl space as they believed someone within the residence must have unlocked the rear door. To their amazement, the house was completely empty. The rear door was key operated from both inside and outside. Officers were unable to locate any keys on scene.

The officers secured the residence and waited for the crime scene investigation unit to attend the scene. When the crime scene technicians showed up, the detectives led them to the rear door only to find that both locks on the door had been engaged. They called for breaching tools, but when one of the patrol officers brought the tools over, the door unlocked again.

The officers re-entered the residence and began another systematic search of the residence. This time, they were sure they were going to locate someone inside the residence. Officers even lifted the beds and emptied the clothes from the closets. However, all search efforts failed to locate anyone.

The body of the deceased was removed from the tree and Detective McGinley departed the scene in order to conduct a death notification to the deceased's next of kin. He was advised by the officer's on scene that the rear door had mysteriously locked on the officers one more time after his departure.

The family attended the scene and the officers told them of the strange happenings occurring with the rear door. This did not surprise the family whatsoever. In fact, they said that the deceased was absolutely fanatical about the condition of the house. He had completely restored the residence to its original historic condition.

Detective McGinley believed that the deceased didn't want strangers in his house but also did not want the police to damage the door. Unlocking the doors only long enough so that the police could fulfill their duties must have been his compromise.

BEAR CORRECTIONAL COMPLEX

In Wallywoo, British Columbia stands the Bear Correctional Complex. The 500,000 square foot prison can house approximately 2,400 inmates. It has been said that this institution may house at least one discarnate spirit.

On a backshift in 2017, Correctional Officer Eugene Adams and three other officers were working in the control room. They were observing the prison's surveillance system monitoring screens while having a casual game of poker. At 2:00 am, Correctional Officer Adams and one of the other officer's looked up at one of the screens and saw a human figure moving across a walkway outside of a row of cell doors. The ghostly figure walked into view of the camera, stopped at the stairwell for a moment and then proceeded to walk past the stairwell. As the correctional officer's watched the monitor, the figure eventually walked off screen. Due to the poor quality of the video feed, the officers were unable to make out any distinguishing features of the person. Correctional Officer Adams and his partner asked the other two officers if they had seen the ghostly figure, but they hadn't.

The correctional officers began to wonder what an inmate was doing out of their cell, as the cells had already been locked down for the evening and no one was authorized to be out. Correctional Officer Adams and one of his partners left the control room to investigate. Three of the inmates whose cells were directly beside the area where the figure had been seen asked Correctional Officer Adams why he was back so soon. The prisoners explained that they had just seen a correctional officer walk only a few short moments ago. This was even more puzzling to Correctional Officer Adams as all of the guards assigned to the housing unit were in the control room at the time they had seen the figure on camera.

Upon inspection, all of the inmates were accounted for and all cell doors were safely secure. The surveillance system had audio as well, but there was no sound of anyone entering or exiting the unit. The housing unit where the figure was seen was the same area where another correctional officer had regularly worked but had died less than a year ago in a motorcycle accident. Perhaps it was the spirit of the deceased guard making one final round at the Bear Correctional Complex that the officers and inmates had so vividly seen.

HAUNTED LITTLE BREWSTER ISLAND

On Little Brewster Island in Boston Harbour, Massachusetts stands the second oldest lighthouse in the United States. This iconic lighthouse was first erected in 1716. The British destroyed the original tower in 1776, but it was re built and lit once again in 1783. Even though the light house became automated in 1998, it is still manned by United States Coast Guard personnel. The lighthouse is operational with its 18 million candlepower lightbulbs and iconic fog horn which both aids and warns seafaring individuals.

As with almost any historic place, Boston Light is not without its tragedies. I learned of this story while on a ghost tour in Boston, Massachusetts with my fiancé, Sarah. On November 3, 1718, the first lighthouse keeper, George Worthylake, his wife Ann, daughter Ruth, servant George Cutler, slave Shadwell and friend John Edge all drowned after their canoe capsized while returning to the island after attending a sermon in Boston. George Worthylake along with his wife and daughter are buried at Copp's Hill Burying Ground under a triple headstone.

After the Worthylake drowning, Robert Saunders, John Chamberlin and a third man named Bradduck were hired as the ad hoc lighthouse keepers. A short two weeks later, on November 14, 1718, Chamberlin and Bradduck both drown while returning to the island after being summoned by a ship entering the harbor.

Since then, it has been reported that many United States Coast Guard personnel assigned to the island have had strange experiences. In 1947, Coast Guard keeper Russell Anderson and his wife Mazie manned the lighthouse. Mazie Anderson reported several strange events.

On one occasion, Mazie was walking the shores of Little Brewster Island when she heard footsteps close behind her. As she turned her head around, there was no one behind her. Later that night while trying to sleep, she felt a presence in the bedroom. She heard what she described as being "horrible maniacal laughter" coming from the boat house.

During another evening, Mazie heard the sobs of a little girl calling "Shadwell" over and over again. During a separate incident, she had seen a figure outlined against the lens of the lighthouse and once again heard the maniacal laughter and sobs of a crying young girl. The Anderson's also reported that the fog signal engines and light would sometimes turn on by themselves.

During the 1980's Coast Guard officer Dennis Dever manned the lighthouse. While on duty in the boathouse, he liked to listen to rock music on the radio. He would often find the radio would change to a classical station. He and the other Coast Guard employees felt that it was George Worthylake himself changing the radio station.

During another shift, Dever was in the kitchen of the keeper's house when he glanced toward the lighthouse tower. Dever saw the figure of a man wearing an old fashioned lighthouse keeper uniform. At the time of the sighting, Dever and his assistant who was in the next room were the only two individuals on the island. Upon investigation, Dever found the lantern room in the tower to be empty.

Coast Guard Petty Officer Joseph LaVigne was the lighthouse keeper from 1948 until 1950. His wife Mary and daughter JoAnn resided with him on the island. JoAnn recalled there being a second floor bedroom that faces the light itself which was always locked. Local legend tells of a lightkeeper during the 1800s that had a wife go insane and murder him around Halloween. The wife allegedly wrote about the murder in her diary. JoAnn stated that every October her family would hear weird noises coming from the locked room. Her mother jiggled the doorknob to see what was going on when suddenly a black image of the lightkeeper's wife came through the door and walked down the hallway, down the stairs and into the kitchen. There was an apparition of a big dog with the lightkeepers wife as well. Petty Officer Joseph LaVigne was away at the time, but his wife called the Coast Guard's sector headquarters in Boston and they dispatched a crew to investigate. They breached the locked door and located the diary of the lightkeepers wife on a pedestal, opened to the night where she had killed her husband. The Coast Guard seized all of the books in the room and JoAnn said that they never heard strange noises coming from that room ever again.

A BROOKLYN HAUNTING

One warm summer evening in 1979, Cst. Jim Blackwood was patrolling a small rural area outside of Clarenville, Newfoundland called Brooklyn. He received a call for service advising that some kids were playing in an abandoned house on Main Road. The complainant was worried that the kids would set fire to the abandoned property. Brooklyn had abandoned houses from when some of the townsfolk could no longer afford to live there. They packed up their belongings and left town.

Cst. Blackwood arrived at the house. He pulled into the driveway and turned off the lights to his police vehicle. He could see a light moving through one of the front windows. He believed that the kids were still in the house and he was excited to catch them. He entered through the back door of the residence which was unlocked.

The inside of the house was completely empty except for a bureau upstairs and a chair left in the living room. It had no running power to the residence. There were signs that the local kids had been using it as a place to go drinking. There were empty beer cans, cigarette butts and garbage strewn about the residence. He had his gun out as he quietly searched each room in the house; however, there was nobody home. He figured that the kids must have run out the front door.

Cst. Blackwood exited the house through the front door and returned to his police car. He was just about to radio dispatch so that he could update them on the status of the file when suddenly he saw a light in the window again. This time, the light was more clear and was emanating from a kerosene lantern. Cst. Blackwood went back into the residence through the front door, but again, he found nobody inside the home.

He told himself "That's it. I don't care if I see any more lights, I'm not going back in there again." Just as Cst. Blackwood was about to exit through the front door, something slammed it shut behind him. There was no wind and the hair on his neck stood on end. He got into his police vehicle and began driving away. As he backed out of the driveway, he saw the light from the lantern appear through the window again, but Cst. Blackwood just kept on driving.

A few moments later the Clarenville RCMP Detachment radioed Cst. Blackwood and told him that they had received a call from the neighbours advising them that there were still kids in the house. Cst. Blackwood said "No there's not and I ain't going back!"

THE RUTHERGLEN POLTERGEIST

On August 8th and 9th, 2016 Police Scotland received calls of a disturbance at a townhouse residence on Stonelaw Road in Rutherglen, Glasgow.

A mother and her teenage son had been residing at the home when they suddenly began experiencing violent and unexplained incidents. The activity had been occurring for two days when they decided that they could no longer take the torture. In a panicked state, they phoned Police Scotland. Initially, the police assumed that they were responding to a mental health issue based on the hysterical phone call and nature of the complaint. However, shortly after the police officers who attended the call for service arrived on scene, that assumption changed very quickly.

Upon arrival, officers witnessed clothing being thrown across a room by an unseen force. The lamps turned off on their own free will and when they turned themselves back on, the lampshades were upside down. The oven door kept opening and closing on its own. Even the family dog, a chihuahua, which was playing outside in the garden upon the arrival of the police somehow ended up sitting atop a seven-foot hedge. Some of the officers with twenty years of service had never seen anything like this before and it left them absolutely perplexed. The mother and her son were clearly in a state of distress.

The officers updated their supervisors who also attended after thinking that the officers were playing some sort of prank on them.

The supervisors for Police Scotland quickly realized that what their officers had been reporting was in all actuality, occurring. Senior officers with Police Scotland were made aware of the strange and unexplained incidents occurring on Stonelaw Road. Although it was a very unique situation, Police Scotland took the inquiry seriously.

With no crime having been committed, by a living person at least, the police sought assistance from the Catholic Church. The Church sent a priest to the house on Stonelaw Road and performed a blessing at the property. Officers made sure that the mother and her son had other relatives that they could stay with. Other than contacting the Church, offering them safety advice and providing them with alternate options on where to live, the police for all intents and purposes were at a loss on how to further proceed with assisting the family. They conducted a background check on the family and assisted in working with doctors and social services in order to provide additional support to the family. They also checked the history of the property to see if there had been any further reports of similar occurrences from previous residents. The historical background check conducted by the police did not reveal anything of significance.

THE EAST YORKSHIRE POLTERGEIST

At #12 Richardson Building on Sykes Street stood one of Hull's most haunted dwellings. It was occupied by James Gilson and his wife Mary. The events in which they endured garnered regional, national and international news attention at the time.

Mary Gilson's brother had recently passed away. He was sick with consumption and had died in her home while laying on a little bed beneath the window in the inner room on the ground floor that led into the kitchen. It was on September 5, 1908 that supernatural activity began occurring at her residence in the early morning hours. Mrs. Gilson did not believe that it was her brother causing the activity as she reported that he was extremely fond of her and they had no rifts in their relationship.

The first event occurred when Mrs. Gilson and her friend Mrs. Grady were making funeral arrangements in the same room in which her brother had passed away. Mrs. Gilson and Mrs. Grady heard a repeated knocking at the door followed by a loud noise as if something had fell in the kitchen. Upon investigation, Mrs. Gilson located a steel comb which had been stored in a comb box. Mr. Gilson and Mary's other brother Patrick heard the noise as well and emerged from the upstairs bedrooms to see what had happened.

All of the witnesses then observed a hair brush fly out of a box and sore across the room. Suddenly a pebble materialized through the closed kitchen door and landed on the floor. Furniture began moving, pots and pans spontaneously flew across the kitchen and the loud sounds of banging and tapping could be heard by all of the witnesses throughout the house. The Gilson's telephoned the local police department.

Initially, Constable Hynes of the Hull Police Force Worship-Street Division, was the first officer on scene. Cst. Hynes walked into utter chaos. There was lots of screaming going on and Mrs. Gilson was so terrified that she fainted. Upon waking, she and her husband had decided that they would stay at the neighbour's house. As Cst. Hynes entered the kitchen, he had an unseen force throw a black box at him from the corner of the room which had just missed his helmet. The black box struck Patrick in his neck which caused him to run out the front door. Cst. Hynes searched the kitchen, but he couldn't find any explanation for what was occurring. The witnesses and Cst. Hynes saw cups and glasses smash when they were thrown by an unseen force. Cst. Hynes searched the entire residence but was unable to explain the mystifying occurrences. He waited outside as he requested the attendance of additional officers. Mr. Gilson and his brother in law Patrick escorted Mary and Mrs. Grady to the neighbour's residence. They returned and informed Cst. Hynes that the mysterious knocking that they had been hearing was occurring intermittently since 3:00 am.

Interestingly enough, there is a general belief that midnight is the "witching hour" of paranormal phenomena. However, in my experience as a parapsychological investigator, activity can occur at any given time. Activity that occurs at or near 3:00 am, is common during a demonic haunting as it is considered to be the "high noon of the demonic day." It is the opposite time of when Jesus Christ died on the cross. Not all ghostly phenomena occurring at 3:00 am should be considered demonic and haunting events should be assessed on a case by case basis.

A strapping young lad named Constable George Cornelius "Con" O'Kelly heard Cst. Hynes request for assistance. Cst. O'Kelly was more than happy to respond. He was a world wrestling gold champion and at the time of the call for service, he had just recently returned from the Olympics. His adrenaline coursed throughout his veins when he received the call. Cst. O'Kelly was prepared to take on whatever was harassing the Gilson family.

When Cst. O'Kelly arrived at the residence, Gilson and his wife had already fled the residence in terror. Cst. O'Kelly and Cst. Hynes searched the residence again, however, the house had become quiet and no further activity occurred while Cst. O'Kelly was on scene.

Despite having witnessed and endured the events herself, Mary Gilson remained skeptical that the events were supernatural. She believed that someone was creating a hoax. However, a thorough investigation was conducted and the only piece of evidence that would suggest that it was a hoax was a walking stick. The walking stick had been located hidden inside a half open window shutter.

Reasonable deduction would conclude that a person using a walking stick would not be able to physically toss a box at the head of a police officer. Mary couldn't have been that skeptical though, because she and Mr. Gilson never returned to the residence and moved all of their belongings out.

THE RUSSIAN POLTERGEIST

Our next poltergeist case brings us to the town of Maraksa, Russia in the Kolpashevsky district. On February 12, 2018 a married couple and their adopted 15-year-old son began experiencing strange occurrences at their residence. A police report written in Russian by police Inspector Alexander Budnik describes the supernatural events that had taken place.

By the time the Russian police attended the residence, the place was in a complete state of disarray. There were household objects lying all over the floor and a knife stuck in one of the walls in the kitchen. The family told the police that they had been enduring the strange phenomena of flying books, kitchenware and furniture by an unseen force for the past two days. The family had also witnessed falling cabinets. Police officers were able to confirm that there was furniture and appliances scattered throughout the house. Police officers witnessed a stick which had flown out of an empty room and saw books fall from a wall mounted shelf. A shelf had also fallen next to one of the police officers. All of the officers in attendance reported the feeling of a presence in which they could not explain. The police report indicates "no rational explanation was found for the specified events."

The police contacted the Kospashevskaya diocese; the Russian Church who would later confirm through the media that everything witnessed by the police and written in their report was true. The diocese sent a priest over to the residence to speak with the family and perform the rite of consecration in the house. The activity diminished upon the priest's arrival, but he would witness objects moving on their own accord prior to the rite of consecration being conducted.

THE BIRMINGHAM POLTERGEIST

In 1981, residents in Birmingham, England were being terrorized by what is known as the Birmingham poltergeist. Someone or something was wreaking havoc on several homes on Thorton Road. Stones would seemingly rain down during the evenings causing significant damage. Many windows were smashed and roof tops damaged. Once a window was replaced, it was once again smashed out by stones. This led some homeowners to build a barricade to protect their property. The Holford residence situated at 32 Thorton Road, house number 34 and the Sidebotham residence at number 36 received the most damage. Some residents even wore tin hats in the event that they would be pelted with stones. The sound of stones rolling off of their roof resonated with residents for many years afterwards.

The occurrence lasted three years and local police Superintendent Baden Skitt assigned Chief Inspector Len Turley to lead a team of police officers to investigate. Chief Turley was confident that he would catch whoever was responsible. Despite Chief Inspector Turley setting up round the clock surveillance which totalled over 1,000 man hours and utilizing specialized police equipment including night vision devices, image intensifiers and automatic cameras, no suspects were ever identified or brought to justice.

Although the police never subscribed to the poltergeist theory, many of the residents did. The stones appeared to always be clean and some described them as being polished. Some residents reported that it didn't matter what room they were situated in, a stone would come smashing through their window narrowly missing them. The police collected hundreds of stones throughout their investigation. They suspected that someone was using a giant catapult to launch rocks at the houses from some 200 yards away. Was it a person seeking enjoyment from the torment and media attention or was it a supernatural occurrence? The Birmingham poltergeist case still remains a mystery some 39 years later.

THE WANDERING SOLDIER

George and Marilyn Morrison lived in Elmvale Acres situated at 2029 Corry Street in a relatively quiet neighbourhood. One of the neighbours recently had their house broken into so residents were paying closer attention to who was coming and going. Corry Street was a U shaped street and the Morrison residence was close to the corner of the street.

On one cold winter evening in Ottawa, Ontario Marilyn Morrison woke up between the hours of 2:00 am and 3:00 am. Whenever her husband George was away on duty with the Canadian Forces, Marilyn would often suffer from a restless night's sleep. Unable to sleep, Marilyn peaked out her bedroom window. She admired the beauty of the freshly fallen snow which was illuminated by the street lamp.

Suddenly, Marilyn saw something moving outside. She saw a figure walking down the street. This peaked her curiosity because it was quite late in the morning for someone to be casually strolling down Corry Street. As the figure walked by her house, she could see that it was a man.

The man was wearing an old fashioned three quarter length thick grey military coat. He was wearing Mountie type high brown boots and had a tilted Stetson on his head. The man wasn't rushing, he was sauntering along. His footsteps disturbed the freshly set snow.

Marilyn initially thought that it was a teenager. She said during this time in Ottawa, kids were purchasing military clothing in second hand stores and wearing it as a fashion trend.

The man kept walking until he reached the curve at the end of Corry Street. At the end of the street stood a discarded snow pile that the plow had deposited there from previous storms. The man continued walking up the snow hill and cut toward the back yard of a residence. The man had now disappeared from Marilyn's sight. Fearing that the man may be looking to do a break and enter, she phoned the Ottawa Police.

A police officer attended Marilyn's residence. She invited him inside her house and provided a description of the man and what she had witnessed. The footsteps were visible to the police officer from Marilyn's front porch, so he decided to follow them. The police officer later returned to Marilyn's residence and told her that he followed the footsteps. To his amazement, there were only two or three footsteps leading up the snow hill at the end of the road and then they stopped.

Marilyn swore up and down to the officer that the man had travelled in that direction before disappearing from her sight. The police officer asked for the description of the man one more time. Marilyn provided him with the same description as before. The police officer responded "You know what? I think you saw a ghost." Marilyn was taken aback by his comments but the police officer further explained that years and years ago the land that Corry Street was built on use to be a military encampment.

Ottawa is certainly known as a government city. A mere three and half kilometers away from 2029 Corry Street is a Department of National Defence building located at 1745 Alta Vista Drive which houses the 33 Canadian Brigade Group of the Canadian Army.

The Elmvale Acres subdivision was developed in the 1950's by Robert Campeau. The land fell within the Gloucester Township which had been established in 1792. I couldn't locate any records that confirmed the military had specifically used Corry Street for anything in particular. I was, however, able to discover that the subdivision and the Department of National Defence building on Alta Vista Drive fall within the City of Ottawa's ward 18, commonly referred to as the Alta Vista Ward. Furthermore, the area has always had a military presence dating as far back as 1853 when the Rideau Canal ceased to be used as a military canal. Nonetheless, the identity of the military apparition that Mrs. Morrison had seen remains a mystery.

THE PRECOGNITIVE DREAM

In 1990, George and Marilyn Morrison travelled to Moscow, Russia to visit their former neighbours Jeff Sallot and his wife Rose-Marie. Jeff was a foreign correspondent and Moscow Bureau Chief with the Globe and Mail.

At the time, Russia wasn't open to visitors but the Sallot's had been inviting the Morrison's to come for a visit. They were scheduled to be posted in Moscow for at least one more year. One day, Marilyn was sitting at home while George was doing a band inspection for the military. The sudden thought of booking flights to Russia overcame her. She called the airlines and made the reservations for her and George to attend Russia for approximately 10 days.

When George called home that evening to check in with Marilyn, she told him that they needed to go to Russia to visit the Sallot's. George told her that they would talk about it when he returned home from his duty. Marilyn said that there was nothing further to discuss as she had already made the reservation.

George called Jeff and told him that Marilyn had booked them a trip to go and visit. Jeff asked when they were coming and George told him they depart in three weeks. "Three weeks!" Jeff exclaimed. Jeff explained that you needed to receive permission from the Russian Embassy and that the wait time is approximately six months. Jeff said he would work on some paperwork from his end but encouraged George to go and see the Russian Embassy to start the paperwork. Jeff warned George that the Russian Government might not admit him entry because he was in the Canadian military.

George and Marilyn went to the Russian Embassy. George didn't believe that their paperwork would be ready in time for their trip. However, three days later, the Russian Embassy called the Morrison's and advised them that they had been approved to visit the Sallot's. Marilyn was convinced that there was some reason that they were supposed to see the Sallot's now. It was totally out of character for Marilyn to spontaneously make a decision such as this without first discussing it with George.

George and Marilyn travelled to Russia to stay with the Sallot's. Jeffrey was covering the after math of the Soviet-Afghanistan war at the time. As a foreign correspondent, he would have to go over there to cover the news. He would covertly fly with another Russian journalist during the evening hours.

Approximately five days into the Morrison's trip, Jeff received a call from work advising him that he had to go to work. The evening before Jeff was scheduled to leave; they had a nice family dinner together. George and Marilyn retired for the evening.

Marilyn woke up during the night with her side of the bed soaked. She had tears coming down from her face and she sat on the side of the bed. She said "Why am I crying like this." She had pictures like on a television rush through her mind about Jeff and his trip to Afghanistan.

George woke up and asked her what was wrong. She was so upset that she couldn't speak. She calmed down enough to tell George about her dream. George knew well enough that whenever Marilyn had a psychical experience such as this, that one should heed her warning. Often times Marilyn would receive the warning three times before the event unfolded. George told Marilyn that she needed to tell Jeff about the dream before he left for work.

Marilyn waited until Rose-Marie was talking to George downstairs. Marilyn spoke to Jeff in his bedroom and told him that she was really afraid for him about his upcoming trip to Afghanistan. Jeff asked her why. Marilyn told him that she had a dream about his trip. She said that she saw him in an open area with palm trees on either side. She also saw a very large ornate building behind him with big brass doors. Jeff was standing with another man behind a little tiny car with its trunk open. She could see Jeff's brief case sitting on the ground. Jeff and the man were looking intently at a map.

Marilyn warned Jeff to get out of the area immediately because something horrible was going to happen. She said she wasn't sure if it was going to be gun fire, but she said it would be something that goes "boom". She told him to run through the building with the big brass doors and to keep running toward the back of the building. Marilyn had tears streaming down her face as she told Jeff about her vision. Jeff believed her and told her to describe the scene to him one more time. She did and she left Jeff with one more piece of advice. Marilyn told him that if he remembered what she had said, and follows her advice, he will be ok. Jeff said that he would remember.

Jeff departed for Afghanistan in the early morning hours. He was scheduled to be there for three days. On the afternoon that he was scheduled to come back to Moscow, Rose-Marie called Marilyn from her work and told her that she had received a call from the Globe and Mail. They told her that there had been an incident where Jeff was reporting from but that he was ok. They said he would be delayed coming back.

When Jeff finally got home, he told Marilyn that he and the guy he was working with had been looking for a particular street. Jeff's partner couldn't find the street on his map because it was so old and it didn't have many street names written on it. Jeff gave his partner his map. They were able to find the street and take care of their business. When they finished, they returned back to their hotel. Jeff's partner said he would be interested in comparing map's to see how outdated his was. Jeff said they could do that before they went into the hotel.

They went to the back of the car and opened the trunk. Jeff opened his brief case and took out his map. Jeff then placed his brief case on the ground next to the car. Jeff and his partner started to look at the two maps together.

Suddenly, Jeff realized that he was standing behind the car with the trunk open and his brief case on the ground. He looked around the parking lot and noticed that there were palm trees on either side of him. He looked behind him at the hotel and saw that it had huge double brass doors. Jeff reached up to close the trunk. He told his partner not to ask any questions, but that they needed to get out of the area immediately and make a run for it toward the hotel as fast as they could. Jeff and his partner began running toward the hotel. They got inside the doors and Jeff told his partner to keep on running toward the back of the hotel. The words were no sooner out of his mouth that Jeff and his partner heard a loud explosion come from outside. An air missile had been dropped and exploded right where Jeff and his partner had been standing.

Marilyn told George that she truly believes that she and he were meant to go to Moscow to save Jeff's life.

MOOSE JAW, SASKATCHEWAN UFO SIGHTING

Retired Master Corporal Andrew Baird spent the majority of his career with the Royal Canadian Air Force as an aerospace control operator. What better witness to a UFO sighting than someone who is trained to survey and control airspace for the Canadian military. Master Corporal Baird's most memorable encounter during his career occurred while he was stationed in Moose Jaw, Saskatchewan.

At the end of August in 2009, he was working an evening shift in the air traffic control tower monitoring some CT-155 Hawks. The pilots were conducting some night time training exercises. Shortly after midnight, Master Corporal Baird looked toward the city of Moose Jaw when he observed a strange bright white light hovering in the night's sky. It looked similar to when an aircraft activates its landing lights. It was the brightest white light that Master Corporal Baird had ever seen. It was a perfect white circle with absolutely no glare. He knew it wasn't a plane because there was no anti-collision lights, and no red flashing lights. He told the other traffic controller about it who checked his traffic sheets, but there was no reported aircraft flying over the city. The air traffic controller told Master Corporal Baird to call the Regina tower. The Regina tower didn't have any indication of any air traffic in the area either. A call was then made to Saskatoon, but they too didn't have anything of significance to report.

As Master Corporal Baird and his co-worker continued to

investigate the strange light, one of the Hawk pilot's radioed the tower and asked about the light in the sky. They updated the pilot advising him that they didn't really know what the light was and neither did any of the other towers. The lead instructor flying one of the Hawks asked for permission to investigate. Permission was granted.

The pilot began approaching the strange light. Once the pilot was about half way to where the strange object was hovering, the light shot straight up into the night's sky and disappeared. None of the military personnel knew what it was.

The object was not showing up on their radar. Their radar was designed to capture both military and civilian air traffic. They called North Bay, Ontario to see if they could play back their radar recordings and see if any objects showed up on their screens. North Bay advised that they did not record any such object over Moose Jaw.

Master Corporal Baird and his partner had to complete an incident report due to the strange and unusual event. They recorded who was present during the incident and what methods of investigation were conducted. The report was then faxed to Winnipeg for further investigation. Winnipeg investigators do not disclose the results of their investigation back to the reporting personnel.

Master Corporal Baird logged the incident in the tower's log book. A few days after the UFO incident, he returned to work. As he was sitting in the air traffic control tower, he began telling a co-worker about the incident which had occurred a few nights previous. He reached for the log book to show his co-worker the entry he had made. To Master Corporal Baird's surprise, the page was ripped out of the book. The only time a page is supposed to be ripped out of the log book is in the event of an aviation accident. Master Corporal Baird never heard anything further about the UFO sighting and it remains unexplained.

NORTH BAY, ONTARIO UFO SIGHTING

While posted to Canadian Forces Base North Bay in Ontario, Retired Master Corporal Andrew Baird had a couple of other UFO encounters. CFB North Bay is also the centre for the North American Aerospace Defense Command (NORAD) operations in Canada only subordinate to 1 Canadian Air Division in Winnipeg, Manitoba.

There were a couple of incidents where objects at approximately 65,000 to 68,000 feet were being tracked validly on the radar. Their speed showed that they were moving extremely slow for aviation being between 22 and 20 knots. When the objects couldn't be identified, personnel were ordered to drop the track.

Commercial flights usually fly between 25,000 to 45,000 feet. The highest flying commercial flight was the Concorde which had the capability to fly at 60,000 feet. Thc Concorde has been retired since 2003. Master Corporal Baird also ruled out weather balloons being the culprit for these radar tracks.

The radar technicians were called out several times to check the functionality of the equipment which was in working order. The technicians did advise that the readings were not caused by reflections and solar flares. These mysterious anomalies were never explained.

HAUNTED HOUSE ON THE PRAIRIES

While posted in Regina, Saskatchewan Master Corporal Andrew Baird founded the Ghostly Eye Paranormal Society consisting of other Royal Canadian Air Force members. After placing an ad on Kijiji, they were called upon to investigate a potential haunting at a private residence in Regina.

A female client told Master Corporal Baird that her great aunt had recently passed away. Ever since her death, the client could feel the presence of a spirit. She lived in a small residence with her husband and their two young children. She reported feeling cold spots and hearing someone occasionally whispering in her ear. The client was scared enough, that she was contemplating whether or not to list her house for sale.

What the client was experiencing are commonly reported haunting characteristics. Thermoception is the ability to dctcct a change in temperature. Both hot and cold spots have been reported during hauntings. Interestingly enough, these changes in temperature are often felt by clients, witnesses and investigators and goosebumps may manifest but the instruments are often unable to detect the change. Auditory experiences that mimic human activity such as whispers and names being called are not uncommon.

Baird and his team attended the residence one evening. The client, her husband and two children were present during the investigation. Baird and his team turned off all the lights, computers and electronics so that there was no electronic interference. Baird confirmed that there were certain areas of the house in which cold spots could be felt. However, their most interesting find came while photographing the residence.

Baird said that anytime they took a photograph of the female client, orangish yellow streaks would be present near her in the photograph. Upon inspection, the digital camera was found to be functioning properly. This only occurred if the female client was present in the photograph.

Unfortunately this was the only evidence collected during this investigation. As with most haunting investigations, they are extremely tedious. The most important tool one can have as a parapsychological investigator is an open but critical mind. Clients who reside at haunted locations have increased exposure to the phenomena occurring than the investigators. There are simply days in which no anomalous activity occurs, even at the most active haunting locations. For this reason, it is important not to discount the client's experiences.

THE FATAL VISITOR

I can attest that fatal traffic collisions are one of the more horrific incidents that a police officer has to attend. The old saying "speed kills" is true. Speed also mangles human flesh and snaps bones. Officers take measurements, photographs, collect evidence and conduct crime scene clean up including looking for body parts that may have been ejected from the vehicle. These types of incidents usually require the roadway to be closed for a period of time.

Constable Catie Rivers, a trained collision investigator received a call to assist the Royal Canadian Mounted Police in a fatal traffic collision. The incident occurred in the winter of 2015 on Highway 101 in Nova Scotia. The highway runs from Bedford to Yarmouth in the Northwest part of the province.

As Cst. Rivers arrived on scene, she acknowledged that it was snowing heavy with large fluffy snowflakes. There was a deceased person sitting in a minivan. Despite the horrific event, Cst. Rivers said she will never forget how quiet and calm the night was. There was no breeze and it was completely black with no natural light or street lamps.

There was a Toyota Corolla down an embankment which had contained two male teachers. They were severely injured and taken to the local hospital by Emergency Health Services. Cst. Rivers said that their vehicle was extremely damaged and that the driver and passenger were lucky to be alive. The vehicle was totaled and the roof had been completely peeled off. The entire interior of the vehicle was covered in blood.

Cst. Rivers climbed down the embankment and held the survey pole at different points so that the RCMP officer she was assisting could take measurements of the Corolla's final resting spot. It was completely dark and Cst. Rivers could only see what her flashlight illuminated.

As she was waiting for further instruction, she suddenly felt a presence with her. All of a sudden, Cst. Rivers felt a hand touch her back and vigorously tug on her traffic vest. She turned around, but there was nobody there. A cell phone began ringing inside the vehicle startling Cst. Rivers even more. By the time she composed herself, she located the phone in the door pocket, but it had ceased ringing before she could answer it.

To this day, Cst. Rivers doesn't know who or what grabbed her traffic vest. She believes that someone or something was trying to get her attention. She has defined this incident as the creepiest moment in her career.

STADACONA

The next story takes us to Stadacona often referred to as "Stad" for short. It primarily functions as a Canadian Forces Navel Engineering and Operations School, but it also contains a Canadian Forces hospital as well.

A young and eager military police officer named Harold Phillips was assigned to Stadacona to do his on the job training in the early 1990's. One evening, the military police received a call that there may be some teenagers partying in the old hospital. The old hospital was shut down and scheduled to be demolished.

The young rookie and some other military police officers arrived at the old hospital. The building was in complete darkness as the power had been disconnected to the building. As the officers made their way through the building on the first floor, they could hear the elevator being operated. The distinct sound of the elevator gears could be heard echoing throughout the building. If that wasn't spooky enough, when the elevator would stop, the sound of the buzzer would "ding" as if someone were getting off the elevator. The officers checked the building but did not find anyone inside.

The military police officers may have experienced what is known as a residual haunting. Parapsychologists believe that energy can be imprinted into the environment causing a scene to replay over and over again like a hologram or video recording. It has been theorized that light particles get trapped and suspended in the atmosphere where they lay dormant until certain environmental factors activate them. None the less, the officers were more than happy to clear this call from their queue.

THE HAUNTED POLICE ACADEMY

The Honolulu Police Department has publicly acknowledged that their Ke Kula Maka'i Police Academy situated at 93-093 Waipahu Depot Street in Waipahu is reportedly haunted. Their training facility opened in 1988 and is used to train new recruits with aspirations of becoming police officers for the Honolulu Police.

Although many Honolulu Police Department officers swear the academy is haunted, very few of them speak openly about it. A security officer working at the academy had his story shared in the local media.

Evenings at the academy are extremely quiet. Recruits are hunkered down for the evening; administration personnel have gone home for the day; and the place literally becomes a ghost town. One evening while conducting building checks, the security officer heard the sound of wood clanking together. As he passed the building where the police canines are housed, they were found to be barking and agitated. As the security officer approached the Special Weapons and Tactics building, he saw all of the wooden shutters opening and closing repeatedly. The security officer noted that there was no wind and as he approached the building the shutters suddenly stopped moving. The security officer couldn't locate anyone on the premises.

A couple of evenings later, the same security officer was working again. As he secured the front gate for the evening, he noticed an old lady dressed in white walking towards him through the parking lot. Thinking that she may need help, he waved toward her, but she didn't respond. As she approached closer, he asked her how she got passed the secured gate, but she disappeared.

The security officer decided to report the incident to his supervisor. As he turned around to radio the supervisor, the lady was standing there. She began approaching him with transfixed eyes and a menacing look on her face. The security officer was taken aback and unable to speak but as suddenly as she appeared, she once again vanished.

The security officer sat down and began collecting his thoughts. As he glanced up, the old lady reappeared for a third and final time. This time she was sitting directly across from him. The security officer had enough fear for one evening. He stood up and ran as fast as possible toward the security office.

HALIFAX, NOVA SCOTIA UFO SIGHTING

The Halifax Regional Police Service has always conducted foot patrols in and around the downtown core. Some of the senior officers I worked with previously told me that while on foot patrol, they would have to telephone their sergeant from a payphone at specific locations and times. If they didn't check in on time, they would be reprimanded. This is a tradition that continues today. Rookie officers are usually required to "walk the beat" for a period of time before graduating to a patrol car.

During the 1970's Cst. Ed Joyce was walking the beat during an evening shift. As Cst. Joyce patrolled downtown Halifax, he stopped at the corner of Morris and Barrington Street. A strange object in the night sky caught his attention. A bright ball of light was travelling overhead along the harbour. Cst. Joyce watched the object travel for a few moments as he was trying to figure out what it was. To his amazement, the object reversed and began returning the same way it had just travelled. Cst. Joyce knew that conventional aircrafts cannot manoeuvre that way and satellites in space can't reserve their direction of travel. It also wasn't a shooting star. Cst. Joyce continued to watch the object for a few moments before it vanished.

As with the majority of UFO sightings, they are reported after the fact leaving very little investigative avenues available to investigators. This UFO sighting was reported to the Center for Parapsychological Studies in Canada on April 21, 1998. The strange light witnessed by Cst. Joyce remains unidentified.

A HAUNTED HOUSE IN TRURO

In January of 1998, retired Royal Canadian Mounted Police Sergeant Ed Malloy was asked to stay at a house owned by a retired RCMP Inspector. The retired Inspector was travelling to Florida on vacation for a couple of weeks and needed a house sitter for his dog. The house was located in Truro, Nova Scotia and was over two centuries old. Surely this would be an easy task for a veteran police officer.

Shortly after Malloy settled in to the retired Inspector's house, he began to notice strange occurrences. The first night that Malloy was there, he was awoken by the sound of the dog running upstairs at 3:00 am. The dog seemed as if something spooked him and he wanted to sleep in the bed with Malloy. He didn't think anything of it and decided to let the dog stay in his room.

The second night, Malloy decided to sleep in the downstairs bedroom. He had a lamp on in the bedroom and all of the other lights turned off. As the evening carried on, he noticed the ceiling light in the kitchen began turning on and off by itself.

The third night, Malloy and the retired Inspector's dog could hear the faint sound of an old fashion wind up siren emanating from the downstairs closet near the front door. The dog's ears were perking up every time Malloy heard the siren. The doorbell began ringing and Malloy saw the outside motion lights turn on. Naturally, he assumed someone was at the door, but when he opened it there was no one in plain sight. This began occurring daily. In fact, it was so disturbing, that Malloy called an electrician in to investigate. The electrician attended but he could not locate any faulty wiring.

Malloy could hear the sound of the downstairs screen door and storm door close as if someone had shut it. He would go investigate, but wouldn't find anyone. He was adamant that all of the windows were shut and that it wasn't a cross breeze.

Even more unsettling, when Malloy was asleep, various items throughout the house would be disturbed. Malloy found blankets pulled back on beds in other parts of the house where the doors had been closed. The retired Inspector would keep the bedroom doors closed so that his dog would not venture into the rooms.

Malloy said that the dog appeared to be aware of the strange phenomena as well, yet was unafraid. On several occasions, Malloy would observe the dog sitting and staring at the staircase. The dog's eyes seemed to be following someone as if they were walking up or down the staircase. Simultaneously, several hanging pictures on the wall leading to the upstairs would swing as if someone had just brushed pass.

One morning Malloy sat at the big country table in the kitchen with his coffee. The table had a blue table cloth on it that he had wiped down the previous day. As he was sipping on his coffee he noticed something white on the table cloth. Upon inspection, it turned out to be a small circle of sugar. Malloy doesn't put sugar in his coffee and he had been the only person in the house since the retired Inspector left for Florida. He could still see the old glass jar containing the sugar sitting on the kitchen counter with the lid sealed shut.

Malloy recalled another strange occurrence. The basement had flooded on him. When he went downstairs, he located approximately 3 inches of water. Even more astounding, was the fact that it was winter and the house was located on top of the hill. He called a plumber in but the furnace and hot water tank were found to be in perfect working order. He vacuumed the water up and dumped it outside, but it kept returning. When he spoke to the retired Inspector, he asked him if he had a problem with his basement flooding, but the retired Inspector claimed it had never happened before. He did know that his house was haunted, but like Malloy, he only experienced non malevolent events.

Malloy said that when the retired Inspector returned from his trip, the activity in the house settled down. Malloy would later find out that the previous owners of the house also knew that it was haunted. Even though the previous owners believed the ghost was friendly, the hired housekeeper refused to work alone in the house.

Unfortunately when the Center for Parapsychological Studies in Canada contacted the retired Inspector to see if they could investigate the claims, the retired Inspector denied that any strange phenomena had occurred at his residence. Retired Sergeant Malloy vehemently stands by his story.

EPILOGUE

After I finished writing my first book, my mother, Kim, immediately encouraged me to write another paranormal book. At the time, I wasn't sure if I would publish a second book, nor did I have any clue what a second book would entail.

The idea for this book arose out of my love and interest in parapsychology and law enforcement. I thought that it would be enthralling to research, collect and present some of the most fascinating supernatural encounters experienced by professional witnesses. All of the stories you just read are true, many of which are being told for the first time.

Rest assured, that each story was researched thoroughly. Don't let some of the stories brevity fool you. In my quest for more information, I wrote to government and law enforcement agencies, spoke to witnesses, recorded interviews and researched historical and modern literature. Some witnesses were unavailable, not locatable or simply ignored my request. Some government agencies refused to release any further information. I am always interested in hearing from anyone who has experienced a paranormal event or may be seeking parapsychological assistance. I welcome you to visit my website for the most recent information about PPRI and myself.

As a parapsychologist, I am interested in phenomenological research design. There were many trends which surfaced throughout this book. For instance, some of the witnesses experienced more than one supernatural event. Some individuals are more perceptive and sensitive to their environments than others. Believers have statistically been shown to have more experiences than skeptics. Another noticeable trend was the lack of propulsion noise during the reported UFO sightings. Professional parapsychological research continues to explicate geographical analysis, statistical analysis, and lived human experiences so that we can continue to understand parapsychological phenomena.

Now that I have completely crossed over into the realm of retirement, parapsychological research and investigation fills the void created when a police officer turns in his or her badge. Interviewing witnesses, conducting investigations and historical background checks, writing investigative reports and educating the public are just some of the parallel skillsets the two occupations have in common. Perhaps in a couple of years, I can present you with a sequel containing all new supernatural encounters experienced by law enforcement. Until then, thank you for your interest in this book. I'll see you again soon, partner.

PARANORMAL PHENOMENA RESEARCH & INVESTIGATION

Paranormal Phenomena Research & Investigation, a non-profit and scientific organization dedicated to serving the public by investigating, researching and providing educational activities in the social science discipline of parapsychology which still has many misconceptions frauds and abusers who misrepresent the field.

PPRI conducts free, ethical and professional paranormal investigations in both the Atlantic Canadian Provinces and the New England States. With over 20 years of experience in this field, we have extensive knowledge, experience and partnerships to draw upon. Investigations remain confidential unless agreed upon by our clients.

PPRI investigators can assist with researching current and historical information on your residence or property. Our organization also conducts its own parapsychological studies.

We at PPRI believe in educating the general public with scientific and factual based information. Our experienced investigators are available to speak to the general public at conferences, symposiums, through media and any other event.

Website:

http://www.ppri.net

Address:

43 Chera Drive

Head of St. Margarets Bay, Nova Scotia, B3Z-0J1, Canada.

E-mail:

info@ppri.net

BIBLIOGRAPHY

ABC News. (2014, September 26). *New Mexico Police Catch Mysterious Ghostly Intruder on Camera.* Retrieved from https://abcnews.go.com/US/mexico-police-catch-ghostly-intruder-camera/story?id=25771690 on April 15, 2019.

Auerbach, Loyd. (2019). *Advanced Field Investigations: Investigating Apparitions, Hauntings and Poltergeist.* Durham, NC. Rhine Education Center.

Bendici, Ray. (2014, August). Lindley Street, Bridgeport. Retrieved from Danced Connecticut on April 14, 2019 from http://www.damnedct.com/lindley-street-bridgeport

Bird, Hilary. (2016, July 28). *N.W.T. Man tells of encounter with Nàhgą – the Tlicho sasquatch – following boat accident.* Retrieved April 9, 2019 from https://www.cbc.ca/news/canada/north/whati-man-nahga-bushmen-encounter-1.3698240

Brunvan, Jan Harold. (1996). *American Folklore: An Encyclopedia* New York, New York. Garland Publishing Inc.

California Digital Newspaper Collection. (1977, April 6). Valley Residents Report More UFO Sightings. Retrieved on August 29, 2019 from https://cdnc.ucr.edu/?a=d&d=DS19770406.2.10&e=-------en--20--1--txt-txIN--------1

Canada's Log People. (2019). *BC Forest Facts*. Retrieved on September 19, 2019 from https://canadaslogpeople.com/about/bc-forest-facts

Cape Breton's Magazine. (1990, August 1). *Mystery at Blackett's Lake by Ronald Caplan.* Retrieved August 20, 2019 from http://capebretonsmagazine.com/modules/publisher/item.php?itemid=3577

CBC. (2014, December 3). *Halifax Shopping Centre to get more stores in $70M makeover.* Retrieved on August 27, 2019 from https://www.cbc.ca/news/canada/nova-scotia/halifax-shopping-centre-to-get-more-stores-in-70m-makeover-1.2859108

Chicago Now. (2015, February 21). *Teresita Basa Killed today in 1977 – Did She Solve Her Own Murder?* Retrieved on September 6, 2019 from http://www.chicagonow.com/chicago-history-cop/2015/02/teresita-basa-killed-today-in-1977-did-she-solve-her-own-murder/

Coast Guard Compass. (2016, October 31). *Growing up at Boston Light: A special and spooky childhood.* Retrieved on October

28, 2019 from https://coastguard.dodlive.mil/2016/10/growing-up-at-boston-light-a-special-and-spooky-childhood/

Correctional Service Canada. (2017, September 12). *Institutional Profiles – Atlantic Region – Dorchester Penitentiary.* Retrieved April 9, 2019 from https://www.csc-scc.gc.ca/institutions/001002-1002-eng.shtml

Correctional Service Canada. (2017, September 12). *Institutional Profiles – Prairie Region – Bowden Institution.* Retrieved April 9, 2019 from https://www.csc-scc.gc.ca/institutions/001002-4001-eng.shtml

Daily Record. (2016, August 15). *"'Poltergeist' baffles hardened Police Scotland officers after they witness paranormal activity including levitating dog."* Retrieved November 4, 2019 from https://www.dailyrecord.co.uk/news/scottish-news/poltergeist-baffles-hardened-police-scotland-8620581

DiRaimo, Hayley and Van Dusen, Elliott. (2019) *Evil in Exeter* La Vergne, TN: Ingram Content Group LLC.

DNA Info. (2016, September 13). *Did Teresita Basa Solve Her Own Murder? True Life Ghost Story Still Haunts.* Retrieved on September 6, 2019 from https://www.dnainfo.com/chicago/20160913/edgewater/did-teresita-basa-solve-her-own-murder-true-life-ghost-story-still-haunts/

Dotson, Michael. (n.d). *Police call in priest to help with poltergeist in Siberia.* Retrieved on November 7, 2019 from https://1428elm.com/2018/02/18/police-call-in-priest-to-help-with-poltergeist-in-siberia/

Exopolitics. (2009, February 1). United Nations General Assembly Decision 33/426 (1978). Retrieved on August 29, 2019 from https://exopolitics.blogs.com/exopolitics/2009/02/united-nations-general-assembly-decision-33426-1978.html

Gloucester Historical Society. (2019). *A Historical Timeline for the Township of Gloucester, Eastview and Rockcliffe Park.* Retrieved from http://www.gloucesterhistory.com/history.html on November 14, 2019.

Gulf News. (2018, June 29). *India: Cops imprisoned by fear of ghosts at 'haunted' police station.* Retrieved August 12, 2019 from https://gulfnews.com/world/asia/india/india-cops-imprisoned-by-fear-of-ghosts-at-haunted-police-station-1.2244145

Halpern, Diane F, Roediger III, Henry L, and Sternberg, Robert J. (2017) *Critical Thinking in Psychology.* Cambridge, UK.

Cambridge University Press.

Harold, Jim. (2014, October 31). *Supernatural Files: The True Story of the Bridgeport Poltergeist Haunting*. Retrieved April 14, 2019 from https://jimharold.com/supernatural-files-the-true-story-of-the-bridgeport-poltergeist-haunting/

Haunted Magazine. (2019, September 8). *The Press, The Police, The Poltergeist & The Piledriver.* Issue 24. Retrieved November 7, 2019 from https://issuu.com/deadgoodpublishingltd/docs/haunted_24_interactive

Hoggard, Brian. (2004). The archaeology of counter-witchcraft and popular magic. In O. Davies & W. De Blècourt (Eds.), *Beyond the Witchtrails: Witchcraft and Magic in Enlightenment Europe*. Manchester University Press.

Hough, Peter and Randles, Jenny. (2001). *Psychic Detectives. The Mysterious Use of Paranormal Phenomena in Solving True Crimes.* London, England. Amber Books Limited.

Hull Live. (2019, October 31). *Hull's creepiest ghost stories including a phantom bottom slapper and hanged woman.* Retrieved on November 7, 2019 from https://www.hulldailymail.co.uk/news/history/hull-creepiest-ghost-stories-halloween-3484550

Journal of Parapsychology. (2015). *Book Reviews – The World's Most Haunted House: The True Story of the Bridgeport Poltergeist on Lindley Street.* Volume 79, Number 2, Rhine Research Center. Durham, NC.

Kelly, E. P. (2012). Trapping witches in Wicklow. *Archaeology Ireland, 26*(3), 16-18. Retrieved from https://www.jstor.org/stable/23320106

KHON2. (2018, November 1). Unexplained ghostly encounters haunt officers at training facility. Retrieved on May 1, 2020 from https://www.khon2.com/news/unexplained-ghostly-encounters-haunt-officers-at-training-facility/

Lederman, Jay. (2013, August 5). *Demons in Bridgeport.* Retrieved on April 14, 2019 from https://patch.com/connecticut/monroe/demons-in-bridgeport

Ledger, Don. (1998). *Maritime UFO Files.*
Halifax, NS: Nimbus Publishing Limited.

Lighthouse Digest. (2000, October). *The Darker Side of Boston Harbor's Lighthouses.* Retrieved on October 28, 2019 from http://www.lighthousedigest.com/Digest/StoryPage.cfm?StoryKey=863

McConnell, Rob. (2011, January 6). *The Shroud of Secrecy Lifted on the St. Catherines, Ontario Poltergeist of 1970.* Retrieved April 10, 2019 from http://xzonenation.blogspot.com/2011/01/shroud-of-secrecy-lifted-on-st.html

Miller, G. Wayne. (2018, September 8). *Are Coventry Cops Chasing Ghosts?* Retrieved on April 11, 2018 from https://www.providencejournal.com/news/20180908/are-coventry-cops-chasing-ghosts

Oickle, Vernon. (2001). *Ghost Stories of the Maritimes. Volume 2.* Edmonton, AB: Ghost House Books.

Parapsychology Association. (2015, November 24). *Glossary of Psi – Premonition* Retrieved on April 12, 2019 from https://www.parapsych.org/articles/53/343/premonition.aspx

Saint Mary's University. (n.d.). *The Patrick Power Library – University Archives – Burke-Gaffney.* Halifax, NS.

Seemit. (n.d.). *The horrified Russian police ask for help form super priests to exorcise a tremendously violent poltergeist of a house.* Retrieved on November 7, 2019 from https://steemit.com/story/@justlikeapill/the-horrified-russian-police-ask-for-help-from-super-priests-to-exorcise-a-tremendously-violent-poltergeist-of-a-house

Smith, Barbara. (2001) *Canadian Ghost Stories.* Edmonton, AB: Lone Pine Publishing.

Somme Branch Legion. (n.d.). *About*. Retrieved on May 3, 2020 from http://sommelegion.ca/about.html

Terrace Standard. (2015, December 28). – *Bigfoot sighting reported in northwestern B.C.'s Nass Valley*. Retrieved on September 19, 2019 from https://www.terracestandard.com/draft/bigfoot-sighting-reported-in-northwestern-b-c-s-nass-valley/?fbclid=IwAR2edCqbNEvDdePKjabiv9elB4xOlSar0nTKs7CCVOE4yZriwefmJyd9Do8.

The Telegraph. (2016, August 14) – *Police contact Catholic Church after baffling 'poltergeist' report.* Retrieved on November 4, 2019 from https://www.telegraph.co.uk/news/2016/08/14/police-contact-catholic-church-after-baffling-poltergeist-report/

Toronto Star. (2013, October 27) - *History of hauntings at Colborne Lodge resurface as Halloween nears.* Retrieved on August 27, 2019 from https://www.toronto.com/news-story/4176168-history-of-hauntings-at-colborne-lodge-resurface-as-halloween-nears/

Tourism Nova Scotia. (2007). *See & Do – Attractions – Point Pleasant Park.* Retrieved on August 24, 2019 from https://www.novascotia.com/see-do/attractions/point-pleasant-park/1461

United States Lighthouses. (2019). *East Coast Lighthouses.* Retrieved on October 28, 2019 from http://unitedstateslighthouses.com/explore-us-lighthouses/east-coast-region/33-boston-light.html

Vernon, Steve. (2009). *Halifax Haunts – Exploring the City's Spookiest Spaces.* Halifax, NS: Nimbus Publishing Limited.

Walsh, Darryll. (2010). *Ghosts of Nova Scotia.* 10th Anniversary Edition. Lawrencetown Beach, NS: Pottersfield Press.

ALSO BY ELLIOTT VAN DUSEN

Evil in Exeter was co-authored by Elliott Van Dusen. This non-fiction story documents the terrifying field investigation into something so sinister that it will cause you to reconsider your belief in good and evil.

Ever since she was a little girl, Hayley has been surrounded by ghosts. As she grew older, she began to realize that no matter where she moved or what place she lived in, the spirits would seemingly follow her. Their presence and mischievous behaviour had never been problematic until she began to realize that something more sinister was at work. Unsolicited warnings by psychic mediums, a failed house blessing by a Roman Catholic priest, and a chance meeting with a Canadian police officer who happened to be a paranormal investigator would uncover an evil that would do anything within its supernatural power to have Hayley for itself.

THE AUTHOR

Elliott Van Dusen is the Corporate Director for Paranormal Phenomena Research & Investigation and Executive Vice President of Ghost Project Canada. After 15 years of service, he retired as a Corporal with the Royal Canadian Mounted Police. Van Dusen has been investigating the paranormal for over 23 years. He co-authored his first book "Evil in Exeter" based on a true story and field investigation involving the terrifying haunting of a Rhode Island family.

He earned a Bachelor of Arts in Criminology from Saint Mary's University, a Diploma in Parapsychology from the Stratford Career Institute, a non-accredited degree in Parapsychology from the American International University and has completed additional parapsychological studies from the Nova Scotia Community College, University of Edinburgh's Koestler Parapsychology Unit and the Rhine Education Center. Van Dusen is currently completing his Master of Arts Counselling Psychology degree through Yorkville University.

He has appeared on The Discovery Channel and in The Globe and Mail, The Chronicle Herald in relation to topics involving the paranormal.

www.ingramcontent.com/pod-product-compliance
Ingram Content Group UK Ltd.
Pitfield, Milton Keynes, MK11 3LW, UK
UKHW041638190726
13854UKWH00006B/2557

9 781999 138523

www.ingramcontent.com/pod-product-compliance
Ingram Content Group UK Ltd.
Pitfield, Milton Keynes, MK11 3LW, UK
UKHW041638190726
13854UKWH00006B/2557

9 781999 138523